The Color of Sabbath

The Color of Sabbath

Proclamations and Prayers for New Beginnings

ROBERT LEE HILL

Hope Publishing House
Pasadena, California

Library of Congress Cataloging-in-Publication Data

Hill, Robert, 1952-

The color of Sabbath : proclamations & prayers for new beginnings / Robert Lee Hill

p. cm.

Summary: "A collection of sermons and speeches given by the head pastor of the Community Christian Church, Kansas City, Missouri, from 1995 through 2007 that gives an overview of how he sees the principles of Holy Scripture and Christianity challenging church members as they interact the with current culture"–Provided by publisher.

ISBN 10: 1-932717-13-7 (pbk. : alk. paper)

ISBN 13: 978-1-932717-13-6 (pbk. : alk. paper)

1. Christianity and culture–United States. 2. Christianity and culture–Sermons. 3. Sermons, American. I. Title.

BR115.C8H54 2007

252–DC22 2007013913

With abiding gratitude and deep affection

for the congregation of

Community Christian Church

in Kansas City, Missouri

in whose esteemed pulpit

it has been my privilege to preach

for the past 20 years

Contents

ASH WEDNESDAY PROCLAMATIONS

CHRISTMAS PROCLAMATIONS

PRAYERS

Introduction

The proclamations and prayers within these pages are proffered with the hope that we might all, preacher and reader, obtain to such a place that there might be, among us all, more experiences of Sabbath. The globe is too strife-riddled for anything less. And most of the people I know are hungry for a greater sense of Sabbath so that they might launch forth into significant, transformative new beginnings. The title for this book is taken from a poem I wrote as part of "a congregation of poems" published in 2003.[1] While there is not included here a sermonic piece with the title *"The Color of Sabbath,"* each and every moment of this book's effort is focused on increasing the presence of *"the sympathy of sepia,/the blessing of blue,/the glory of grey,/ the yes of yellow,/ the belief of brown,/ the rest of red,/ the peace of pink,/ the gladness of green....."* A world too often shadowed by back-and-white dramas of catastrophe and made anemic by colorless calculations to treat people as less than they are, stands ready, I believe, for the call to *"Behold rainbows"* and to *"be whole,/ be made whole,/ be healed."* Imbued by the color of Sabbath, we might be better equipped for some much-hoped-for new beginnings.

No sermon or prayer is ever uttered in the abstract, that is, without a context. Thus the *"Times and Places"* for each entry can be found at the back of the book.

No sermon really happens without a text. And so, all proclamations in this volume, except for two, have been listed with the texts tied to the respective preachments or meditations.

Most of the sermons herein have been presented within the worshiping embrace of the family of faith at Community Christian Church, in Kansas City, Missouri. Some have traveled beyond that pulpit to other venues. A few have happened in a situation totally other than what happens regularly at the corner of 46th Street and Main Street in the middle of the greater Kansas City metropolis.

Speaking of *"Main Street,"* there is a sense in which each of the *"Main Street Proclamations"* is intended to reach beyond the *"Main Street"* that courses north and south through Kansas City, Missouri – what many people have called *"in the heart of the heart of the country"* – and to land somewhere on the *"Main Street"* of each reader's life.

The *"Ash Wednesday Proclamations"* and *"Christmas Proclamations"* are clearly connected with those respective holy days on the Church's liturgical calendar. It has been a refreshing experience to come upon such premier days of Christian awe – one that commences the Lenten season of sober reflection and the other that culminates the Advent season of watchful waiting with the fulfillment of Christmas' joy – and find the preaching moment so free-flowing. It is sheer gift to be afforded the opportunity to be of use in those sacred occasions.

In all circumstances it is a daunting and yet blessed task to attempt to be of use with words, spoken or written. It is my hope that these words can be as much of a blessing to those who receive them as it has been to the one who initially rendered them. And may they serve as a fervent invitation for new beginnings.

Notes

1 *"The Color of Sabbath," **Hard to Tell: A Congregation of Poems, 1990-2003*** (Los Angeles: MOSAIC Impressions, 2003), p. 25

Acknowledgments

As always, and as I have said on many occasions, the laboratory of love that is Community Christian Church is a blessing to me. I am deeply grateful for the encouragement and enthusiastic welcome given by Community's members for the proclamations and prayers within this book. It is within Community's congregation that the rainbow colors of sabbath have been made most manifest for me as a preacher and as a person of faith.

I abide with an unpayable debt to Community's staff, Cynthia Weaver and Janet Fiebig in particular, whose sharing of the past two decades' worth of ministry has been cause for ongoing celebration. To Mary Reliford, I am especially thankful for her careful editorial eye and for her selfless support of the messages and the messenger.

To the ministerial colleagues at Community with whom it has been a delight to share life over the course of time when these proclamations and prayers were uttered–Richard Woodard, Troy Sybrant, Joan Bell-Haynes, Jerry Porter, Donna Muiller, Amy Lignitz Harken, Dara K. Cobb, Tom G. Haley–I remain grateful for their grace-filled ways.

Debts are owed to several preachers along the path leading up to this book. I heard Ivan Dugan's preaching before he even baptized me. Roy Daniel's preaching was always tinged with encouragement, joy, and the promise of love. Denton L. Roberts' whose pastoring excellence imbued an abiding trust in the efficacy and genius of church and his preaching at my ordination launched me on my way as a minister of the gospel. Pat McGeachy, sermon upon sermon, graced so many hearts and souls, including mine, with words more fitly spoken than those which many have ever heard.

To Ron Allen, Eric Belt, Chuck Blaisdell, Forrest Church, Emanuel Cleaver, J.D. Cooper, Mike Graves, Alvin Jackson, Holly McKissick, Pete Larson, Gay Reese, Kim Gage Ryan, Brent Schondelmeyer, Don Schutt, Gary Straub, Kris Tenny-Brittian, Yolanda Villa, Johnny Wray, and Michael Zedek, I say thanks for generous (and often overwhelming) support all the way home.

And to Priscilla, beloved and best critic, there are endless gratitudes to express. She knows best the tone of love in the color of sabbath.

A Poem as A Preface

The Color of Sabbath

In an early morning dream,
two faces speak fluently,
asking for identity and origin.
"Are you Asian or Caucasian,
African or Indian or what?"
"You mean my ethnicity?"
"Yes, your place of beginnings,
how you come to have that color."
"Well, I guess you could say that
I am the color of Sabbath."

Do not conjure
oil or acrylic,
chalk or water color hues.
No stains or pallors or shades,
no pentimento,
only tints and tones
borne by hand and
through the face and
around the mouth and
in the iris of the eye.

"I am the color of Sabbath."
See and receive–
the sympathy of sepia,
the blessing of blue,
the glory of grey,
the yes of yellow,
the belief of brown,
the rest of red,
the peace of pink,
the gladness of green.

Behold rainbows
and who I am,
and be whole,
be made whole,
be healed.
Keep my face close,
keep me close to your face,
and then, as I am,
be consecrated, and say
"I am the color of Sabbath."

Main Street Proclamations

1

Living Beyond Fear:
An Open Letter to the Candidates

Texts: II Chronicles 7:14 and Ezekiel 28:16-17

Dear Candidates:

A mere six weeks from this coming Tuesday, we, the people of the United States of America will, once more, with vigor and purpose, exercise our rights and responsibilities as citizens, as we select a host of newly elected and re-elected officials as leaders of our nation, our states, our counties, and our municipalities. Premier among our selections will be the person we choose to occupy the Oval Office in the White House for the next four years. Customarily, a message such as this would be tendered to the *newly* elected President, some time after the election and before the day of inauguration on January 20th of 2005. Yet, the tenor of the times and the burdensome concerns with which many are bothered inspire me to offer this communication today. To wait until the turning of the new year would seem to be, at best, an evasion, and, at worst, cowardice. We face too many momentous issues during a time of war and in the midst of war-like politics to remain silent.

So, greetings from Community Christian Church, and, as we say in our tradition, *"Grace, mercy, and peace from God the Father and Christ Jesus our Lord"* (1 Tim. 1:2). After the example of Paul, we Christians are urged to offer *"supplications, prayers and thanksgivings...for all [people], for kings and all who are in high positions [such as presidential candidates], that we may all lead quiet and peaceful life, godly and respectful in every way"* (1 Tim. 2:1-2). But, let us note quickly, in these days of uproar, it is difficult to lead a "quiet" life; in this time of war and rumors of war, it is hard to lead a "peaceful life"; in this season of contentiousness and division, it is nigh unto impossible to know how to share "godliness" and "respect" in any lasting way.

As your respective campaigns proceed forward to the first of the debates this coming Thursday, it is good, we believe, for you to know at least four realities about those of us here in this congregation, and some opinions we hold about ourselves in "the heart of the heart" of America.

- ***The kingdom of God will not rise or fall on Nov. 2.*** The kingdom of God–the in-breaking realm of God's justice and mercy–does not depend on this or any other election. It should behoove religious people and political operatives of all kinds to quiet their rhetoric in this regard. The apocalyptic tones and the scare strategies in some speeches–regarding the choice of one candidate over another–serve only to horrify and humiliate. They do not ennoble or enlighten. To suggest that the choice of one candidate over another will weaken our nation and make us more vulnerable to future terrorist attacks is a despicable and reckless statement. You all and we can and must do better than such rhetoric.
- ***There is no such person as "God's candidate."*** It is certainly not illegal (and is, in fact, commendable) to appeal to

religious folks to vote their consciences (as citizens of obvious and perceived moral convictions). But to equate any sort of righteousness with a certain way of voting is a desecration of the spirited diversity that infuses most congregations, especially ours, and a dishonoring of the time-honored separation of church and state. On November 2, Christians–along with Jews, Muslims, Hindus, and all other religious people, for that matter–will be casting votes for a variety of candidates, aligned with a variety of political parties. While we may adjudge that certain candidates align more harmoniously with our values than others do, there is no one person–man or woman or child–who is "God's candidate." Anyone who suggests such a notion joins forces with the vestiges of a malevolent past and the hurtful wounds over which a World War was waged.

- And, likewise, ***human opinions are human opinions.*** We would not say, during this or any other political season, that any of our individual, human opinions are truly ordained of God. Our convictions emanate from our faithful and fallible lives, not from some ineffable inerrancy under our inviolable control. We each have been given brains and hearts and souls by which to discern, as best we can, the most appropriate policies and candidates. But ours are preferences, not prophecies of pre-ordained realities. It is good, in this regard, to recall Abraham Lincoln's sentiments 140 years ago. At a White House dinner, so the story goes, a pious, churchly gentleman offered a benediction, closing with the affirmation: *"The Lord is on our side."* When President Lincoln did not respond to this sentiment, someone asked him, *"Mr. President, don't you believe that the Lord is always on the side of the right?"* To which Lincoln retorted, *"Sir my concern is not whether God is on our side. My great* *concern is to be on God's side."*[1]

- ***Grace, not works, always marks our territory.*** As we seek to be more and more on God's side, we need to declare that ***ours is truly not an ownership society.*** Yes, we know that one of the greatest accomplishments in many an American life is to own a home. And, yes, young adults take exceeding pride in that "first car" they truly possess. But who owns the daylight that shines on every face? Who owns the gravity that keeps every foot planted on the ground? Who owns the will to freedom and the expression of grace in daily human life? Who truly owns the inspiration that sets us racing pell-mell down hallways of justice and corridors of joy? Who owns the virtues by which we strive to live better and better lives each and every morning? Who owns the impulse to worship and to pray and to live a truly impressive ideal: "kindness in the absence of gain."?[2] Who truly owns what finally matters? Can we ever forget, do we *dare* ever forget the wise counsel of the Psalter: *"The earth is the Lord's and the fullness thereof..."?*[3]

Now to the situation in which we middle-of-the-country Americans find ourselves. It is like unto the situation that Tyre and its princely ruler faced when Ezekiel prophesied a challenging word six centuries before Christ's birth. After a long series of oracles–pertaining first to the siege of Jerusalem (chapter 25), and then to the offending Ammonites (chapter 26), and then to the entire jingoistically prideful lot of Tyre's population (chapter 27)–the prophetic word finally bursts forth from Ezekiel about Tyre's prince himself. It is both an address and a lament about the actions and attitudes of the prince, summed up with this damaging description: ***Your heart was proud because of your beauty; you corrupted your wisdom for the sake of your splendor..."*** Of course, and thankfully, we no longer must abide a theocratic monarchy, as did the people of Tyre under the prince of Tyre. But the parallels between Ezekiel's time and circumstance are eerily parallel to ours. Has our American heart been too "proud" because of our "beauty"? Have we corrupted our "wisdom" because of our "splendor"? Can we ever imagine coming close to such failings and falling away from the true purposes of freedom and freedom's ways?

Beyond Ezekiel's insight into the corruptibility of power, we recognize that we all face a base-level of "free-floating fear" these days.

We are ***frightened*** by the specters of increasing violence at 27th and Prospect in Kansas City, Missouri, *and* just around the corner in *way* too many of our neighborhoods all across our metropolis.

We ***worry*** about things we cannot change and are over-wrought, over-worked, and over-concerned about the things we can.

We experience ***guilt*** in the face of that which we could have made better or right and didn't.

We are ***insecure*** when we wonder if we can ever do or be *enough* to measure up to someone else's standards.

And we are made far too weak by ***dreary dread*** about the basic limits of life–the fact that we can only be in one place at any one time, the fact that we have but only one earthly life and that it does not go on forever.

But there is more. We are haunted by the daily theme of fear itself. We have forgotten what President Franklin Delano Roosevelt proclaimed in 1933, and what President Ronald Reagan cherished a generation later as a constant watchword for the American people: *"The only thing we have to fear is fear itself."* In the place of such a confidence the fears that have nagged our nation and haunted our world since the tragic events of 9/11 continue to plague us. And any President who would lead us effectively will always, necessarily work toward the quickening within us a recollection of "the better angels of our nature" to dispel such fear.

As for solutions in our situations, what are we to say? And what will you say? And, more importantly for us people of faith, what does God's gospel of love, mercy, justice, and peace say about our prospects?

We have sure guidelines for followers in the Judeo-Christian tradition. There is a great assurance granted to Solomon upon the completion of the Temple at Jerusalem: ***"...if my people who are called by my name humble themselves, and pray and seek my face, and turn from their wicked ways, then I will hear from heaven, and will forgive their sin and heal their land."*** President Bush and Senator Kerry, we pray that you will commit yourself to our highest ideals and the practical wisdom passed on to Solomon...

- *The call to simple humility* is clear – for both of you and for us all. A sense of humility – a humility that we can see in your eyes, & detect in your manner & observe in your leadership – shall always be in order.
- *Prayer and worship* are always in order and when we do more of both – fully mindful of current events and how God's gospel of love applies to them – whole communities, whole states, whole nations, and indeed, a whole world will benefit.
- *Turning from our wicked ways*, now that's a different story. Such a turning will be difficult indeed, since many of us are so prone to avoid any description of anything we ever do as "wicked." And well we should, since the world is too overly full with Calvinistic self-loathing and enmity. But an honest assessment of our failures, individually and corpo-

rately, and heartfelt repentance of spirit are always in order when a great nation wants to become even greater.

Our times now are not unlike a difficult time in the past, when, in the torpor and torment of the roiling 1960's, the great rabbi Abraham Joshua Heschel sent an urgent telegram to the Oval office, urging then President Kennedy to recognize and act with courage in an hour that called for ***"high moral grandeur and spiritual audacity."*** Such an hour has once more arrived.

How tragic are the potential consequences when we fail to act with moral courage. Such a moment occurred two weeks ago, on a quiet Monday morning, with seemingly not much going on legislatively in our nation. But shame on us and shame on our national leaders, all across the board, on both sides of the aisle! I grew up in a hunting culture. I shot a shotgun when I was eight years old. I have many friends who enjoy hunting. To me three of the most wondrous smells in the whole world are: (1) the smell of my wife Priscilla's hair, (2) the aroma of a cup of coffee brewing in my own kitchen; and (3) the scent that emanates from a spent shotgun shell. I treasure the friendships I have with respected folks who are life-long members of the NRA. But how on God's good green earth is it justifiable to put our police officers, highway patrol officers, FBI, CIA, and Security forces are greater risk, by allowing the ban on assault weapons to expire? How pathetic that there was nary a whimper from any of our leaders. Shame on the members of the House and the Senate for caving in to the perceived threat of a powerful lobby. And shame on us for electing such examples of cowardice.

As for winning the peace, it should be admitted that whoever wins the election come November 2 will enjoin one of the most daunting challenges to be faced by a President and a Congress – Winning the Peace. From all reports, from both the Department of Defense and from the UN, from anecdotal accounts by soldiers whom we continue to support strongly with our prayers and our earnest hopes, from assessments by trustworthy journalists and wizened military strategists, the prospects for a "best case scenario" in Iraq have now nearly vanished. It is clearer every day that we are learning all over again a lesson which has been taught throughout our journey as the greatest democratic republic in the history of the world: democracy best develops as a percolating reality from the bottom up and from the center of a people's culture. It falters, sometimes tragically, if imposed from above and/or without.

As I send this message your way, I am mindful of a list of service men and women posted at the entry way to our church building. We have prayed for these individuals, and indeed all the service folks in Iraq and Afghanistan and other places where they have placed their lives in harm's way for the cause of the United States. To us, these are not abstractions on some statistician's count, nor are they only a roll call of the valorous, as valorous as they are. They are members of Community's family of faith and the sons and daughters and husbands and wives and uncles and aunts of members and friends of our congregation who requested prayers for them. I would like you both to know their names: Spec. Johnson Kincaid, Capt. Heather Shuey, Lance Corporal Trent Shuey, Corp. Jonathon Bent, Joshua Schafer, Guy Michael Radcliff, Sgt. Kyle Thorne, Commander Tony Mitchell, Priv. 1st Class Brian Ensor, Justin Klaus (MP Army), 1st Lt. Matt Rupnick, SFC Mickey Hartsook, Staff Sgt. Jaudon White, Major Richard Klein, Jason Bernard, Keith Taylor, Paul Haddock, Rebecca Weaver, Shawn Skaggs.

And Mr. Bush and Mr. Kerry, whoever prevails come November 2, make fast your plans and make sure your resolve to bring them home, bring them home. Out of the pain of 9/11, a line of connection between the Afghanistan endeavors and the containment of terror was assumed. Then there was the presumption that the "Iraqi Freedom" cause would be and do likewise. But less and less, we admit, do we see the connection between what has ensued in Iraq and the prospects for defanging the serpentine capacities of any terror network. Out of the pain of 9/11 and out of the wisdom gained since Baghdad was overtaken and Saddam Hussein was captured, may you help us all heal with a return of our soldiers to friendly shores and our embracing arms. Yes, we know that the sine qua non of political life is purposeful strength, but equally important is the sine qua non of religious life which is compassionate love. May you each have large portions of both.

Recognize, President Bush and Senator Kerry, that for too many of our brothers and sisters in the United States, this is now a despairing and despicable moment.

Instead of growing toward what Josiah Royce called ***"the beloved community,"*** we have become be-deviled isolates. Instead of building what Martin Luther King called the ***"new world house,"*** we have grown satisfied with the old, dilapidated apartments of our petty prejudices. Instead of abiding in the ***strength to love*** which is given by God, we have become addicted to the love of strength which is given by the world.

The protection needed is for all, because as President Kennedy proclaimed in his inaugural address: *"If a society cannot help the many who are poor, it cannot save the few who are rich."*

May our hopes and dreams for our common future not become so much refuse–like the red, white and blue placards that will litter the medians of our cities and the front yards of our neighborhoods across the country on November 3: merely yesterday's slogans defunct of any consequence.

When the election is over, one of you will be ***our*** President. And as bitter as the political battle has been, and regardless of how wounded our hearts (and our egos) may be, we pledge to unite our hearts and minds as people of one nation.

Speaking of our nation, let me note one final thing. While you each seek the Presidency, neither of you will ever ascend to the highest office in the land. The highest office-holders in the land are those singular, distinguished, and blessed individuals who each bear the name "citizen." As occupants of the highest office which can be obtained in a democracy, we citizens pledge to work together – while not in total agreement then still at least with a shared fidelity devoted to the common good – for the betterment of the United States. As Christians, we pledge to work together with all who will join us for the increase of life and liberty in a world sorely in need both, as well as freedoms' goodness and God's grace. May it be so. AMEN.

Sincerely yours, just as surely as each of you and we all are sincerely God's,

Dr. Robert Lee Hill, Senior Pastor, Community Christian Church

cc: Emanuel Cleaver, Candidate for Representative, Missouri's Fifth Congressional District

Jeanne Patterson, Candidate for Representative, Missouri's Fifth Congressional District

Senator Christopher Bond, Missouri Senatorial Candidate

Missouri State Treasurer Nancy Farmer, Missouri Senatorial Candidate

Notes

1 (http://www.indianchild.com/abraham_lincoln.htm)

2 The phrase is Betty Lou Donaldson's

3 Psalm 24:1

2

The Gospel & 'The Da Vinci Code'

Texts: II Timothy 3:14-17 and I Corinthians 4:1-5

Today we begin a new series of Sunday morning messages under the overarching theme of ***"Making the Gospel Real."*** I'm excited about this new series of sermons, as we connect the timeless power of the gospel to the timely issues of our day. The current array of pressing concerns, especially those which connect with aspects of popular culture, offers us brand new ways to share the gospel. Through this series, we will discover again that the Christian faith is a spiritually trustworthy path that is, as one poetic cleric in New England put it some 225 years ago: ***"as considerate of persons as the teachings of Jesus; as devoted to justice as the Hebrew prophets; as responsive to truth as science; as beautiful as art; as intimate as the home; and as indispensable as the air we breathe."***[1]

Now, I would remind us that the Chinese ideogram for "crisis" is made up of two characters, one meaning "danger" and the other meaning "opportunity." Today, we take up the gospel in connection with the runaway best-selling novel *The Da Vinci*

Code by Dan Brown and the famous blockbuster movie by Ron Howard as an ***opportunity*** for learning and growth. Dan Brown's book enjoys a top-ten ranking on most bookseller lists, now some three years after its debut. And who can argue with the prolific nature of this pop culture phenomenon? There are 43 million copies of Dan Brown's book in print,[2] and Ron Howard's movie will surely rake in at least a half billion dollars before the movie goes to DVD.

We are taking a look at *The Da Vinci Code* because it provides us an ***opportunity*** to sharpen our understanding of the basics of the Christian faith as informed by the Bible and the history of the Church. Some commentators have pointed out the unusual alliance between two groups whose basic approaches to faith are traditionally mutually exclusive: fundamentalists and the Catholic Church. *The Da Vinci Code* is offensive to each group, I believe, for different reasons. For fundamentalists, *The Da Vinci Code* challenges the notion of "the inerrancy of Scripture." For the Catholic Church, *The Da Vinci Code* challenges the hierarchical authority and integrity of the Catholic Church itself. Since most mainline Protestants and significant numbers of evangelicals are troubled neither by the necessity of Scriptural inerrancy nor by challenges to the hierarchical authority of the Catholic Church, books and movies like *The Da Vinci Code* become for us opportunities and not dangers.

There are so many questions that have been asked in relation to *The Da Vinci Code*: *"Is this true?" "Did the Bible come to be in the way that 'The Da Vinci Code' says it did?" "Was Mary Magdalene really married to Jesus?"* And more!

Brown's novel prompts such questions in a better-than-average "whodunit" format, with a focus on Leonardo da Vinci's dazzling painting of *"The Last Supper"* and the search for "The Holy Grail." In the course of his 454 page page-turner, Brown raises intriguing questions about how the Bible came to be, the relationship between Jesus and Mary Magdalene, and the development of the Church.

The characters are rather simple; the plot is rather complex. Twisting and turning in an on-going sequence of clues and riddles having to do with Leonard da Vinci, his art work, and his supposed membership in a secret society, the storyline involves "Robert Langdon," a Harvard "symbologist," and "Sophie Neveu," a French cryptographer, as they seek to uncover the murder of the curator at the Louvre (described at this early juncture in the story as Sophie's grandfather), found naked and mysteriously sprawled near the Mona Lisa. Along the way there's a seeming titan of encyclopedic knowledge named "Teabing" and an albino monk assassin named "Silas" punctuating the plot's action with their nefarious doings.

Before proceeding much further, I need to say something quickly about the nature of reading novels and the upshot of *The Da Vinci Code.* Don't fret, I'm not going to give away the plot's conclusion, lest I spoil a fairly good read and/or movie for those who haven't yet discovered *The Da Vinci Code*. Rather, I want to point out that *The Da Vinci Code* is a work of fiction, an imaginative leap meant to entertain.

Or let me put it another way, with an illustration from a reporter. Each summer, a *Washington Post* columnist runs a listing of notable T-shirts observed on the beach at the Ocean City, Maryland.[3] ***"I child-proofed my house, but they still get in."*** ... ***"Buckle up. It makes it harder for the aliens to snatch you from your car."*** Some have to do with how crazy life is: ***"My reality check just bounced."*** ***"Earth is the insane asylum of the universe."***

There are some very good ones about identity, who one is and is not: ***"I'm not 50. I'm $49.95 plus tax"*** ... ***"I'm not a*** *snob. I'm just better than you are."*

And, of course, there are some for cat devotees: *"It's my cat's world. I'm just here to open cans."* ... *"We got rid of the kids. The cat was allergic."* ... *"Cats regard people as warm-blooded furniture."*

But my favorite is one that you chocoholics will adore: *"Every time I hear the word 'exercise,' I wash my mouth out with chocolate."*

Allow me to add one that can be worn on the beach in Maryland or in the Plaza in Kansas City or anywhere else in America: *"The Da Vinci Code: It's Fiction!"*

What *The Da Vinci Code* does do, and does so plentifully, is weave a story that has implications for the Church (the Catholic Church in particular) and for our common understanding of the Christian faith in general. Unfortunately, as one commentator has stated, *"Brown's approach seems to consist of grabbing chunks of his stated sources and tossing them together in a salad of a story."*[4] By the way, as many of my clergy colleagues are well aware, there is a boatload of commentary about *The Da Vinci Code* available. Two of the best books about the novel are Brandon Gilvin's *Solving the Da Vinci Code Mystery* and Greg Jones' *Beyond Da Vinci.*[5]

Throughout the novel, there are questions about the veracity of the New Testament. For example, there is the claim that the Emperor Constantine squashed all but his own version of the Bible in the year 325. Which isn't true, given historical evidence that shows that the canon of the New Testament was in formation beginning in the first century of the Church's existence, and that the canon, as we have it today, was formulated in 387 CE.

The Da Vinci Code further claims that the Holy Grail was not the legendary chalice from which Christ drank at the Last

Supper, and for which the mythic round table knights labored, but rather the actual person of Mary Magdalene, who was married to Jesus and with whom she had a child. The sacred relics of her bones are objects of considerable interest throughout the latter parts of the story.

About the questions which *The Da Vinci Code* raises for us as Christians, I want to point out three key themes in Dan Brown's book and Ron Howard's movie that run counter to the essential, basic teachings of the Christian faith.

Secrecy

If *The Da Vinci Code* is about anything, it is about secret knowledge and secret ideas contained in secret documents, and that secret knowledge and those secret ideas being carried on through the centuries by elite secret societies. Yes, the Knights Templar was a group that existed, but it was disbanded by the 14th century.

Yes, Opus Dei has existed and even exists today, but, according to all trustworthy sources among respected scholars, both liberal and conservative, not in the way *The Da Vinci Code* depicts it.

The books of the Bible, and particularly the words of Jesus in the New Testament, do not focus on secret knowledge and secret codes for the secretly privileged. The gospel isn't about secrecy but rather about ***mystery***. Christians are, says the apostle Paul, ***"servants of Christ and stewards of God's mysteries"*** (1 Cor. 4:1).

There's a world of difference between secrecy and mystery.

A secret has to be kept. A mystery, while ultimately impenetrable, is in plain view.

A secret is coded. A mystery is written in the language of everyday life.

A secret can harm, if not kept or shared or protected rightly. A mystery can heal, and often does, when it is shared widely and warmly with one and all.

Only a select few are privy to secrets. Mysteries may be encountered by the multitudes.

Conspiracy

Conspiracies, as conspiracies always do, run wild in *The Da Vinci Code.* There are so many in *The Da Vinci Code* that it's really hard to keep track of them all. That may be part plot device on Brown's part, to keep you plowing through the chapters.

But it's also the nature of the beast called "conspiracy." (And before you say it, let me say it for you: *"Well, just because you're paranoid doesn't mean that they're* **not** *out to get you!"*)

In contrast, except as a metaphor, "conspiracy" is not a word that fits easily into the repository where the Church keeps its best words. Instead of conspiracy, the Church focuses its life on – that is, it lives, breathes, and has its being by virtue of – God's spirit moving in and through the gathering of Christians in ***community***.

Community, the very name for our family of faith, is what Christ was and is all about, which any intelligent reading of the New Testament and any insightful interpretation of his message and meaning will show. We may want conspiracy, but Jesus offers what his followers – from the first disciples down to us – know to be the essence of his message: "the kingdom of God is among you"...in *COMMUNITY*!

Duplicity

Another, final "main issue" that *The Da Vinci Code* raises about the Church and Christian faith, is the matter of duplicity. In the course of the storyline, one of the characters proclaims, ***"Almost everything our fathers taught us about Christ is false."***

There is the notion that Christ's divinity was a matter of a duplicitous vote in a church council.

There are also the declarations that: (1) the beloved apostle situated next to Jesus in Leonardo da Vinci's "Last Supper" masterpiece is actually Mary Magdalene; (2) the Early Church Fathers tried to suppress this knowledge and other extraordinary variances from traditional understandings about Jesus and his followers; and, (3) subsequently, Da Vinci knew this and tried to convey it – in coded fashion – in his art.

In the face of these charges, and others, allow me to offer some categorical responses – based on ***truthful complexity*** – to some of the more pressing questions many of you have sent my way since you picked up *The DaVinci Code* (and ripped through it like a hot chain saw through butter) or went to see the movie:

** *Did Jesus and Mary Magdalene have children out of wedlock?*

** *Did Jesus and Mary Magdalene get married?*

** *Did Jesus and Mary Magdalene create a bloodline of inheritors detectable today?*

** *Did the Catholic Church in conspiratorial secrecy connive to suppress this "knowledge"?*

** *Is there an explanation other than the one Dan Brown offers for the formation of the Bible and the New Testament?*

The answers to these questions, according to the best of historical and Biblical research are "No," "No," "No," "No," and "Yes." From all reliable documents we have at our disposal, Jesus was never married, and he didn't have children. I say that in faith, as one can only say it when you're dealing with documents nearly 2,000 years old. I also say it with confidence that the truth of Jesus' life and teachings are found in the Bible and among the followers who have walked after him – by the billions! – in the light of his wisdom, mercy, and saving grace.

What we have in the Bible are testaments, and about Jesus specifically, a ***new testament.*** And the main testament for Christians is not about a secret being transmitted to only a select few, but the wholesale sharing of a dependable truth: the love of God is made manifest and eternally real, available, livable in Jesus Christ. In short, ***Jesus gives us a way of life–resplendent with possibilities for joy, reconciliation, growth, community, fulfillment, hope, forgiveness, justice, mercy, and transformation–and then he bids us to give that way of life to others.***

Some folks want Jesus to be more like us, let's face it. That would solve a lot of intellectual problems. We want Jesus down on our level–to tame him, perhaps, to domesticate his radical ideas, maybe. Maybe it's just so we can get close to him. But Jesus doesn't stoop to our level. Fully human, fully divine, as Irenaeus reminds us, Jesus tenders a loving invitation to us in order to raise us up to his level.

So, not duplicity, but truthful complexity. Not a fiction created as the figment of someone's imagination, but rather the testimony of those who were touched in a loving, chain-reaction of grace by the presence of Jesus of Nazareth, not only theoretically in the world but actually in their lives.

Now about the Bible and how it came to be, let me offer three brief observations that are extremely important to note.

Three Criteria for adjudicating the placing of the gospels in the Bible

Taking into consideration some suggestions from John Ortberg, who echoes most contemporary scholarship, here's the "AAA" test for the overall process for how the Bible came to be as we have it today and especially the basic criteria for how a gospel came to be included in the New Testament. (And even though Ortberg, as an evangelical, and I, as a mainline Protestant, hardly hold to the same theological posts, we do share a conviction about these solid principles for assessing the validity of the gospels and their placement in the New Testament.)

(1) ***Antiquity***–Ancient authorship.

(2) ***Apostolicity***–Approximate closeness to Jesus' apostles, and, then, next, those closest to the apostles.

(3) ***Acceptance*** and common use by the early church at large.

The Bible as we have it is very nearly like the scriptures that arose among the first followers of Christ as the Church in his name was taking shape. They were confident in the time of Paul's missionary journeys that the sacred writings–i.e. the Hebrew Bible, for the first followers of Christ–were trustworthy, dependable, and powerful enough to instruct Christians in the ways of a righteous and lovingly graced life before God.

In II Timothy, the Church heard a truth it would stake its life on: "*...**from childhood you have known the sacred writings that are able to instruct you for salvation through faith in Christ Jesus. All scripture is inspired by God and is useful for teaching, for reproof, for correction, and for training in righteousness, so that everyone who belongs to God may be proficient, equipped for every good work.***"[5]

Conclusion: An Ineffable Mystery!

Allow me to close with a word from a wise soul, one of the wisest souls ever, who long ago gave an assessment of how we can ascertain the veracity of statements about who Jesus is and the claims and power of his gospel. A classical musician, a medical doctor, and a philanthropist par excellence, Albert Schweitzer was the first theologian in modern times to set out on a quest to debunk the past, to get at the actual historical facts and figures that could, somehow, anneal the seeming hurt that science and other disciplines of human reason had done to

Christianity's claims. Long before any of the members of the New Hermeneutic folks rallied around the "God is dead" flag (and attempted to unfurl its myriad meanings), and long before the Jesus Seminar chose any color of beads to cast their votes for what truly are (or are not) the authentic sayings of Jesus of Nazareth, there was Schweitzer. In addition to bequeathing to the world the marvelous phrase, *"reverence for life,"* Schweitzer set all modern followers of Christ on a "Quest of the Historical Jesus," the name which he gave his massively important book one hundred years ago. In short, the good Dr. Schweitzer, at the last from Lambarene, Congo, is the "grandfather" of all the modern movements to delve into what really happened at the time of Christ and how we can really know who Jesus was and is.

At the end of his ground-breaking book, Schweitzer concludes that clinging to Christ is a matter of faith. Christ is made real, not by the vindication of a stack of incontrovertible evidence, but by believing in Christ's truths *despite* the lack of factual evidence. On the last page, in the final paragraph, there is this, which is an answer to any fiction such as *The Da Vinci Code*, about the matter of how we relate to the carpenter from Nazareth and his meaning for our lives: ***"He comes to us as One unknown, without a name, as of old, by the lakeside, He came to those who knew Him not. He speaks to us the same word, 'Follow thou me,' and sets us to the tasks which He has to fulfill for our time. He commands. And to those who obey Him, whether they be wise or simple, He will reveal Himself in the toils, the conflicts, the sufferings which they shall pass through in His fellowship, and, as an ineffable mystery, they shall learn in their own experience Who HE is."***[7]

So, enjoy the book. And enjoy the movie. And remember: they're fiction. And remember too, what the Christian faith is about: not secrecy, but mystery; not conspiracy, but community; not duplicity, but truthful complexity. AMEN.

Notes

1 The First Congregational Church, Lee, Massachusetts, lays claim to this smart adage as emanating from their "Founders".

2 The tallies for sales keep mounting. Compare the ranking by David Grainger ("The Passion of the Da Vinci Reader," *Fortune,* March 4, 2004 issue, http://www.fortune. com/fortune/articles/0,15114,593670,00.html) and the most recent status of *The Da Vinci Code* on *The New York Times* paperback best sellers list.

3 Many thanks to Karl Roscoe for this bit of T-shirt humor. The application, for better or worse, is all mine.

4 Sandra Miesel, "Dismantling The Da Vinci Code," *Crisis* magazine, September 1, 2003.

5 Brandon Gilvin, *Solving the Da Vinci Code Mystery* (St. Louis: Chalice Press), 2004; and Greg Jones, *Beyond Da Vinci* (New York: Seabury Books), 2004.

6 II Timothy 3:15-17

7 Albert Schweitzer, *The Quest of the Historical Jesus*, 1906, p. 401

3

The Resurrection and the Life: Easter

Text: John 11:25-26

Wow! What a gracious moment this is! What a glorious morning to be alive. Easter is here, and we are called to celebrate. And there are few words better to utter this morning than "Wow!"

There's nothing quite like the momentous and overwhelming joy of worship on Easter Sunday. It is the supreme homecoming, the final reckoning, and the absolute graduation exercise. It is the best party, the utmost reunion, and the grandest symphony. It is the definitive victory, the ultimate prize, and the chief satisfaction of humanity's deepest longings. Easter is all these realities and more, because of one simple yet mystically dynamic reality: resurrection. The apostle Paul said it best: *"If Christ is not raised, then [our] faith is futile."* But I get ahead of myself. More on the resurrection in just a moment.

First, we need to ask, "What is Easter...for all of us?

For some, this is...

A Morning of New Life—New life is now, finally, breaking

through the resistance of a hardy winter. And that new life is now burgeoning all around and throughout our yards and gardens and parks. Easter is centered upon the fact of new life which God provides for all creation and which God can offer all individuals.

For others, this is...

A Morning of Happy Celebration–You know how much I have emphasized this reality with you time and again: ***Life is not meant merely to be tolerated, it is meant to be celebrated!*** Tim Whitmer has it exactly right and knows this! And Tim knows what you and I also know: there is no greater time for celebration than Easter. Celebration is why we augment our Easter musical proclamations with beautiful brass orchestrations, and jazz vocalists, and powerful choral compositions. And even though some folks enjoy being curmudgeons, there is something in us all that prefers smiles to scowls, good times to bad, the sweetness of celebration to the bitter dregs of degradation. In short, don't we all like to party, even just a little, more than we like to frown?

For still others this is...

A Morning of Optimistic Feelings–The central thesis of the Easter reality is, we like to assume, we can overcome the appearances of a Good Friday world with an Easter faith. Because love overcomes all obstacles, and because new life abides as a real possibility for all people, there is all the reason in the world to have optimistic feelings. "You can make it, you can make it, I can make it, we all can make it, this is what Easter's for." Right? Well, maybe in part but never all together. Easter is so much more.

Lately I've to put together some Easter metaphors, similes, and comparisons. Let's see what you think?

Easter is...

...as clear as the horizon at the first glint of dawn...
...as gentle as a baby's cheek...
...as undeterred as God's great turning of the earth upon its axis...
...as revolutionary as you forgiving yourself...
...as saving as the words "I love you"...
...as crucial as your next gulp of air...
...as sumptuous as the best comfort food you've ever known...
...as comfortable as clover on a spring day, on a hillside, with blue skies above and the blanket of a soothing breeze over you, and only thoughts of good tomorrows on our mind...
...as lightning-quick as a Quik Trip cashier making change...
...as cool as the other side of the pillow.

Pretty good, huh? Well, not nearly good enough, I'm afraid.

What the New Testament gospelers all agree on is that Easter is about ***none*** of the above. Instead Easter is about the resurrection. *"While the virgin birth, miracles, and the teaching of Jesus appear in some New Testament books and are missing in others, faith in the resurrection is common to all"* (*The People's New Testament Commentary*, p. 101).

Now the various accounts of the resurrection are impossible to harmonize into a congruent whole. They differ and diverge in significant ways.

Mark's gospel is a kind of *"stop-and-go, go-and-stop"* gospel, in that three women go to the tomb, and there are no appearances of Jesus. And they flee in fear.

Matthew is sort of the *"increasing appearance"* gospel, according to the unique way he tells the resurrection story, as Jesus appears first to two women at the tomb and then later in Galilee to all the disciples.

Luke tells it differently still, in a *"kaleidoscopic way,"* jumping from place to place, with three specifically named women going to the tomb (in addition to another unnamed woman) with no appearances to the women but appearances to two guys on the road to Emmaus. Then Jesus appears to all the disciples at once.

John's gospel tells it in a "*he-called-my-name*" fashion, as he has Jesus appearing tenderly to Mary Magdalene on Easter morning near the tomb setting, and then to ten disciples (minus Thomas, to whom he will appear later), and then to the eleven disciples one week later. Then, in a kind of denouement, he appears to seven of the apostles in Galilee.

Now among all of our assumptions and investigations of all the gospel accounts of the resurrection, one fact must be focused upon and admitted: In none of the gospel accounts is there an eye-witness description of the actual resurrection itself. None. If you can find one, they'll likely create a new category and grant you a Nobel Prize for Religious Genius Work for the year 2006.

Which means that the resurrection remains a mystery. Which means that perhaps the most appropriate approach to Easter is one of awe-struck wonder rather than dogmatic domination. Instead of whooping up on the rest of the world that may not hold to our belief in the resurrection of Jesus – "*Hey, hey, look at us world! Our guy won, we can prove it!*" – it behooves us to remember the responses of the apostles and take care to abide in humility as we join our voices in declaring that Jesus is raised from the dead.

So what is resurrection?

Is it renewal? While renewal is always preferable and ultimately needed in our family life, job situations, and school endeavors, and social circles, resurrection is always more than renewal.

Is it rejuvenation? While rejuvenation is, of course, absolutely required for our physical bodies and our emotional well-being, resurrection is always more than rejuvenation.

Is it restoration? While restoration is appropriate for relationships as well as for buildings, and while restoration of one's sense of wholeness and integrity is essential, resurrection is always more than restoration.

Is it revival? While revival is ever and again a much-needed experience in churches, and neighborhoods, and individuals, resurrection is always more than revival.

Is it resuscitation? While resuscitation happens not only in hospitals, gently tendered by doctors, nurses, and other health care workers, resurrection is always more than resuscitation.

No, resurrection is different than these alliterative, synonymous possibilities. Resurrection, to put it simply, is the "always more" of God's grace and love.

Some folks believe erroneously that the Christian faith is about the immortality of the soul, about what *we* can accomplish beyond the threat of debilitation, despair or even death. But resurrection is so much more than that. Resurrection is not really about immortality. Immortally is more a philosophical statement about the possibilities of human nature. Resurrection, on the other hand, is about God and God acts on the behalf and for the benefit of those who are dead. Which is why, in John's gospel, Jesus can proclaim the resurrection and his absolute identification with the resurrection nearly nine chapters before the crucifixion takes place.

In his seventh and last sign in John's gospel, Jesus revives and resuscitates Lazarus. And he does so, in order to point to that which is "always more": his (Jesus') resurrection that will be unlike anything the world has ever seen. Jesus was obviously a close friend of Lazarus and the two sisters Mary and Martha.

And surely his love for them compelled him to raise Lazarus in a fashion that was utterly unique. But it was in order to show a sign about Jesus' own resurrection. When Martha nearly chastises him for being two days late in responding to Lazarus' trouble, Jesus simply responds "Lazarus will rise again."

"Oh I believe in the so-called resurrection," you can nearly hear her say, "and I know that our brother Lazarus will ultimately rise again, in God's own time. But that time isn't here yet."

"Oh yes it is," Jesus says in essence, with what must have been a searing glance that touched her to her soul. And then he utters the greatest *"I am..."* saying in all of John's entire gospel: *"I am the resurrection and the life."*

Now the word for resurrection in the New Testament is *αναστασισ* (*anastasis*), meaning "against stasis." Against the static, the stultified, the staid, the stuck. It is part of Jesus' plan to raise up Lazarus as a sign of his own raising, only Jesus' raising will be a resurrection, beyond all stasis.

And Martha sees what he means. When he asks, "Do you believe this?" you can hear in her words an unwavering answer, a reply touched with awe-filled grace: "Oh yes, I see. I can see farther than I've ever seen before. I can see all the way to what looks like the beginning of a glimpse at the first dawning of what might be eternity that is beginning *now*!"

For Martha and Mary, and for us, what Jesus says about his being the resurrection mysteriously transforms all worry and anxiety into faith and gladness. What Jesus is as the resurrection will change those who were "no people" into "God's people."

And Jesus as the resurrection, then in his own time and for generations forever thereafter, will lift up the downtrodden and embolden those who have been used, abused, or confused. In real time the power of God's love rolls the away the stone of despair so that we all might walk forth into a bright daybreak of merciful hope. In this scene Jesus reveals God's ultimate prescription for the sicknesses of a strife-riddled, war-torn, speed-driven, power-addicted world.

Through the presence of Christ at Lazarus' tomb and then through God's powerful presence at Jesus' tomb, resurrection is the great testimony that love's incessant truths always outlast the deceptions of death. Through the resurrection, the *via dolorosa* becomes the *via gloriosa.* The way of sorrow becomes the way of glory. Which is a great thing, in and of itself. But if that's all Easter is about, then we can put away the trumpets and silence our celebration and file out of here with no further ado.

Over the last couple of weeks, a lot of you have been asked me about the newly published *"Gospel of Judas."* Allow me to say a couple of things quickly about it, which may illuminate also something about the trouble with merely resting on the first half of Jesus' statement about being "the resurrection..."

The gospel of Judas is like the gnostic gospels that came before it. The first mistake that gnostic gospels make is ***denying the significance of the body in preference for the spirit.*** In the gospel of Judas, as I understand it thus far, there is a consistent miscalculation that physical matter doesn't really, ultimately matter as much as spirit. Which is a wholesale affront to the notion of the incarnation, and the fact that we live in this world, and that, as John's gospel says it so beautifully for us on Christmas Eve, *"The word became flesh..."* Gnostic gospels always deny such a radical identification with human flesh. And the gospel of Judas is consistent with that mistake.

The second mistake the gospel of Judas makes is in holding to ***"salvation through secrecy."*** Gnostic gospels are predicated on the basis of a "secret insight," a "secret wisdom," a "secret knowledge" all of which only a few select folks can know. Notice the opening lines of *"The Gospel of Judas"*– *"The secret account of the revelation that Jesus spoke in conversation with Judas Iscariot."* And there never was a bigger lie. ***All*** of the gospel accounts announce that they are open to public, in varying ways and with varying angles of interpretation, so that ***all*** may know and believe and ***all*** may live in the ways of Jesus.

In an argument in support of an embodied life and in support of an "open secret" accessible to all, John's gospel has Jesus saying that he is "The resurrection...***and...the...life."***

Meaning? If we believe in the resurrection, we're all in for an "extreme makeover!"

Meaning? When we engage in our ritual greeting of "Christ is risen! Christ is risen indeed!" we are declaring that God has granted victory over all obstacles. God's love conquers any thing and every thing that would attempt to demean or debase the goodness of creation.

And this remains true even after the tumultuous triumph of Easter Sunday. After the lilies have wilted, after the crowds have ebbed and diminished away, after the last "Hallelujah!" has receded into a faint echo, there is still reason for holding on to hope. Because when Easter has come, when it really hits home in our hearts, nothing ever remains the same.

Easter means that we not only have the blessed gift of an entry into a life beyond death, but in this day, in this existence, ***Jesus gives us a way of life–resplendent with possibilities for compassion, caring, justice, mercy, forgiveness, reconciliation, and fulfillment–and then he bids us to give that way of life away to others.*** It means we can stop trying to seek out and secure only what we don't have and can instead receive what God has already given us.

John Fowles (famous for his novel *The French Lieutenant's*

Woman), once described *"that desert-making heresy that happiness is having what one lacks."*[1] This is our problem these days–isn't it?–seeking after what we think we don't have in order to feel or pretend that we're all right? When we engage in such desert-making heresies, *"an age of self gives way to another age of hell."*

Resurrection is about the heavenly experiences that are also available in ***this*** life. What if we took that way of life that Jesus first gave us and gave it away each day? It might be like this candle. When I light the other candle, my candle doesn't diminish in any way shape or form. In giving my light away, it fulfills a broader function, a higher destiny, a greater fame.

Living the resurrection is what Jesus is talking about when he announces "I am the resurrection and the life." Which is exactly what Breanna Morey knows all about.

Just recently, I received a gift package with a loving note in it. *"This bag of Easter candy is given to each resident of Edgewood Manor with love and compassion from Breanna Morey,"* the note read. It went on to say Breanna's age and mentioned her living in Raytown where Edgewood Manor is situated. Then her note stated, *"As part of [Breanna's] Pastor's Class in 2005, all the children in the class are asked to perform a service project. The children decide as to what the project will be, tell the minister what it will be and have one year to complete the service project. Breanna knew almost immediately that she wanted to do something for a nursing facility. When her grandfather was recently admitted to Edgewood Manor for therapy following back surgery, she said right away that she wanted to do Easter candy bags for the residents. Breanna is a member of Community Christian Church, 4601 Main Street, Kansas City, Missouri 64112...Breanna delivered 70 bags of candy for the residents with 55 bags of regular candy and 15 bags for diabetic residents to enjoy. The staff is welcome if extra bags are left."*

As you can imagine, the residents of Edgewood Manor love Breanna. And, after the gifts and her visits with every resident in all 70 rooms there, they loved to see her coming to visit her grandfather. Not because of the candy, though that was sweet, literally and metaphorically. Because, instead, Breanna witnessed to them about her faith in a loving God. She continues to visit with them, and show care for them, and be a sign of the resurrection and the life, even to this day. Even though the residents there may experience pain or osteoporosis or Parkinson's or Alzheimer's or congestive heart failure, there is a bit less anxiety about this life and the next.

Now Breanna Morey knows a lot about what Christ's resurrection means. She's living it. That's why I call this bag of candy which Breanna left for me, "Sweet, Sweet Resurrection Candy." She's living the resurrection and the life.

As is my mother-in-law Christine. As you know Christine had to evacuate out of New Orleans at the end of August as Hurricane Katrina approached. New Orleans is her home, beyond questioning or debate. New Orleans is the town she was born and raised in, where she was married, where her husband, Priscilla's father, Raymond Towles Reckling, died. Where she had spent, until this year, every Thanksgiving and every Christmas holiday of her life. And as spry as she looks, she has some maturity on her, 85 years of it. So you have to know something of the sense of loss she experienced. She's doing fine, though, so please no outright or subtle expressions of pity, either of which she would shun in a nanosecond.

She's living in a caring community, with plenty of activities and outings and contact with Priscilla and myself to suit her. And this is so, even as she attempts to soothe her grief over the losses, the deep, deep losses she has known because a horrifying hurricane swept away the livability of 285,000 homes in the greater New Orleans metropolis. Beyond her grief, and in keeping with her new life and her steadfast, forward-tilting inclination into the world, there is a look in her eyes. William Edwin Orchard, one of the greatest and most curious ecumenical Christians who ever drew breath called it *"this strange light in our eyes."*[2]

Inasmuch as Orchard died before I was ever glint or glimmer in either of my parent's eyes, I was never able to ask Mr. Orchard straight away what he exactly meant. But it's meaning is there, it's really plain after all, in the end. *"This strange light in our eyes"* is the resurrection look. And that's the look Christine has in her eyes. Beyond the debilitation of her house on Atherton Road. Beyond all the loss of connection and sense of place and grieving over the plight of those far worse off than she is, there's this look, this strange light, this light of "the resurrection and the life" in her eyes. And when I see it, I know not only that she's going to be all right, but that we all will be so with her, and that all will be well. I believe I've seen it in Breanna's eyes. And I've seen it in your eyes, too. And when I see it, all I want to say is *"Hallelujah!"* And also *"Christ is risen! Christ is risen, indeed!"*

So, *"Hallelujah!"* and *"Christ is risen! Christ is risen, indeed!"* Happy Easter, and as we behold the strange light in one another's eyes, please know that I love you. AMEN.

Notes

1 John Fowles, *Poems*, (New York: Ecco, 1973)

2 William Edwin Orchard, *The Temple: A Book of Prayers* (London: J.M. Dent & Sons, 1913)

4

Columbine: Crisis & Christ in Colorado

Text: Romans 12:9-21

Remembering

I will not soon forget where I was on April 19, 1995, and I doubt if you will either. I was right here in the sanctuary when I heard the horrific news about the terrible tragedy at the Murrah Federal Building in Oklahoma City.

Last week, while I was attending the Board of Directors meeting of the Christian Church Foundation, I experienced a similar sort of horror. I will not soon forget, if ever, the moment on April 20, 1999, when Jim Johnson, the Christian Church Foundation president, announced to those of us in the LaGuardia Conference Room at the Holiday Inn that a shocking calamity was unfolding in Littleton, Colorado. I remember now and I will remember for quite some time, with perfect clarity, where I was sitting, whose face I was looking at, whose voices were speaking, and the terrible sense of tragic return.

The heinous rampage by Eric Harris and Dylan Kliebold was a painful reminder of where we have been, as a culture over the past few years. The killings at Columbine High School in Littleton, Colorado, reminded us with a crushing cruelty how little we have progressed in learning from the lessons of previous debacles. Do you recall them? It wasn't that long ago, really. Pearl, Mississippi. West Paducah, Kentucky. Springfield, Oregon. Jonesboro, Arkansas. That's where we were supposed to have been. Back then. Past. Gone. No more. But here it was again, reminding us of Santayana's greatest truth: "Those who do not learn from the past are condemned to repeat it."

And Littleton, Colorado, triggered other serious and tragic events across the greater Kansas City area. More than a dozen threats of one sort or another have caused school clearing and closings. A minister colleague of mine in Oklahoma City reports: "On the day of the [Columbine] shooting a young 15-year-old boy at Sante Fe High School in Edmond [Oklahoma] was arrested for having a 'hit list.'...[And on April 23rd] Memorial High School in Edmond couldn't hold class until noon because of a bomb threat that kept the kids out of school...-Then, on Wednesday [of this past week], a young man in Alberta, Canada stormed into his school in a blue trench coat carrying a gun. When the attack was over another student lay dead in the halls of learning while another was wounded."[1]

The news media cried out our anguish with bold headlines: "Why?" asked *Time*. "Why?" again asked *U.S. News and World Report*. "My God, My God!" said *People*. "The Monsters Next Door," claimed *Newsweek*. And possibly the most striking juxtaposition of all, making a declaration about our status in the great anthropological chain of being, came from *The New York Times*. At the top of the front page of last Sunday's issue was a stark picture of the impromptu memorial that had sprung up near Columbine High School with the title, "Menacing 'Trench Coat Mafia' Was Just a Joke, at First," followed by a story about a scientific find just below, "Discovery Suggests Humans Are a Bit Neanderthal."

Those headlines tell us where we have been and where we are. They are an all too familiar echo of what we have known to be true across the United States: we live in perilous times and our brokenness is excruciatingly painful. Our own experience of crime, particularly the deaths of more than 30 children and youth by gun violence in 1998 here in Kansas City, once caused us to pronounce the same words that were uttered so frequently since the Colorado nightmare occurred just ten days ago: "We never thought something like this could happen here." No one, no place is immune from the dangers of these perilous times. Consider the word that has come from The National Center for Victims of Crime:

- During 1996-1997, there were about 11,000 incidents of physical attacks or fights in which weapons were used and 7,000 robberies in schools that year.
- About 190,000 fights or physical attacks not involving weapons also occurred at schools in 1996-97, along with about 115,000 thefts and 98,000 incidents of vandalism.
- Over the five year period from 1992 to 1996, teachers were the victims of 1,581,000 nonfatal crimes at school, including 962,000 thefts and 619,000 violent crimes.
- Since the mid-1980's the rate of murder by youth has doubled, increasing to 102%.

And The Center for Disease Control and Prevention has reported:

- In the United States, homicide causes 20% of all deaths among youth and young adults 10 to 24 years of age.
- 1350 youngsters carry guns to school every day.

All of which goes to show us that, for the whole nation, "we may have come over here and arrived on different ships, but we're in the same boat now."

Is there a word from the Lord?

In the face of such events, and at such a time as this, you have placed a mantle of responsibility upon me. You have been asking, as you should, as the people of God have always asked down through the ages, "Is there a word from the Lord?" Is there something that our faith can say in response to this tragedy in Littleton. "Is there a word from the Lord?" Is there something we can do, faithfully so, to heal, to learn, to grow from this catastrophe? "Is there a word from the Lord?"

The mantle has been burdensome, to be sure. I cannot recall a more difficult time in preparing a message for any previous worship service here. I cannot remember losing such sleep as I have lost these past ten days. But with the grace of God, including the overwhelming grantings from what Gardner C. Taylor calls "a sanctified imagination," a word from the Lord did come. In fact it has been here all along.

The apostle Paul put it this way: "Do not be overcome by evil, but overcome evil with good." To the early church at Rome in his delineation of the "Marks of the True Christian," Paul concludes this momentous portion of his most densely theological work with a simple imperative: "Do not be overcome by evil, but overcome evil with good."

What we need now is a way to implement such an imperative, to understand how to live out such a charge.

So, with your permission I want to offer "Five Proposals for Parents by the Church." And then mark down "Ten Commitments by the Church to Our Youth." (I should, at this time, pay due attention to the debt I owe a young friend of mine, Shelley Anderson, who lives in Littleton, Colorado. She is the daughter of one of Priscilla's best friends. From my perch, I would describe Shelley as one of Priscilla's precious God-daughters. Shelley goes to Arapaho High School in Littleton, yet she has heart-felt connections with the Columbine High School students. Just this past weekend, Shelley described to me how the Arapaho students had collected enough money for the Columbine girls soccer team to purchase new uniforms. Shelley's insights and good vision and sensitive sophomore heart have informed my interpretation of the Paul's word from the Lord.)

Five Proposals for Parents by the Church:

(1) **Let the adults be adults.** Parents, guardians, and all caring adults have a responsibility and sacred duty to lead, guide, show, and maintain a good world for children. So let the adults be the adults. You have a right to say "Because I said so." Young children and teenagers are in need of boundaries and limits, and look to adults to show them where those boundaries and limits are. So let adults be adults.

(2) **Let us turn down the volume of violence in our lives.** And by the volume of violence, I am indeed referring to what should be called by its rightful name: "Hate radio." Radio and television programs which attempt to foment hatred among groups, enmity between certain opponents should be turned down and out. The vehemence and enmity fostered by hate radio is paralleled by road rage and expressions of anger everywhere, in all modes of media. Now, I confess, this presents a terrible dilemma for me. I'm beginning to wonder, seriously wonder, if I should stop allowing violence into my system when I attend a movie by the likes of Bruce Willis, Arnold Schwarznegger, Sylvester Stallone. You know the movies. And, perhaps like me, you've found them tremendously gratifying. Just plain fun sometimes. Blow-em-up, rock-em-sock-em movies. Yeah! But maybe, as an example to others, and possibly as a discipline for my own spiritual health, maybe such media

should no longer be allowed into my system as entertainment. Let us all turn down the volume of violence in our lives.

(3) **Let us cultivate communities where friendships flourish.** Religious communities can be the sites of some of your most beautiful and caring friendships. Do you know that some of the deepest and most abiding relationships that you can experience happen in church? It is in church where differences can be respected and honored. It is in church where individual talents can be appreciated and celebrated. Cliques never fare very well in church. Because we are an Easter people, there is the possibility of connections, community and friendships for the loneliest of the lonely, for the most dejected of the dejected. I like the story of told about William Booth, the founder the Salvation Army. During the Boer War, a hungry group of people gathered to discuss the distribution of a small amount of food that was left. Each church group, it was agreed, would attempt to take care of their own. An Episcopalian said, "All of you that belong to my denomination come with me." A Presbyterian said, "All you Presbyterians come with me. A Baptist offered the same invitation, "All you of my denomination, please follow me." Then William Booth, the quiet unassuming Salvation Army rose and said, "All you fellows and gals who belong to nobody, follow me." The church is in the business of creating communities where friendships are fostered and flourish. As adults, let us create such communities for our youth, for one another, for everybody, and for all those who belong to nobody.

(4) **Let us establish service as premier virtue and treasured value.** Let us lift of community service and involvements to help mothers so that we all – children, youth, adults – can

maintain a proper perspective about our daily existence. It has been shown that there is little index or correlation whatsoever between violent behavior among teenagers and community service performed by teenagers. That is to say, if a teenager, if adult, if anyone, is regularly involved in helping others, in creating a better community for others and themselves, they are highly unlikely to be involved in violent behavior, crimes of various sorts. Let us establish service as premier virtue and treasured value. Which now leads me to one that you adults may not like very much but we need to here this, I believe...

(5) **Let us as adults simply listen to our youth.** Simply listen. If we will listen, we will likely find ourselves avoiding the temptation of stereotyping our youth. We will come to better know them as the precious human beings they are. Another way of putting it is to say that we adults are to H.U.S.H. That's an acronym for Helping...Understanding...-Supporting...Holding. As adults helping our job description in relation to our youth. Understanding is what they are yearning for the most. Support is what we are charged with, from tennis shoes to breakfast to daily encouragement. And Holding is something we can all do a lot more. Today, I encourage you to hold those children and youth you cherish with a fierce affection. For when you hold them you actually participate in a premier theological doctrine, namely "incarnation," the word of God's love becoming flesh in our midst. Let us as adults simply listen to our youth. Let us "H.U.S.H."

Ten Commitments To Our Youth & the Youth of the Nation

Now let us venture our commitments to our youth, and indirectly to all youth everywhere in this nation, really. These are heartfelt. Let us commit ourselves to making all these commitments for the health and healing and hope-filled futures of our youth.

(1) **We will love you!** No matter what, we will love you. You may try to get us to not love you, but it won't work. You may not like certain folks, including adults, especially including your parents from time to time, but we will still love you. And certain adults may not like you from time to time, or they may not like certain of your actions, but we pledge that we are going to love you no matter what.

(2) **We will honor you!** We will honor your feelings, your considered thoughtful opinions, your perspective on things. We will attempt to keep church, as well as school, as well as home and city hall and all the rest of the public venue places, as safe and secure dwelling places for you.

(3) **We will support you.** That's the task of adults: to support our youth with the rudiments of nutrition, shelter, comfort, and care, so that they will mature at a reasonable rate and experience healthy growth. Stylistically speaking, you may not get everything with a designer label on it, but we promise to support you with clothes that will serve you well, practically speaking.

(4) **We will do all in our power to see that weapons of mass destruction, such as the TEC-9, are eliminated from society.** (Perhaps I push too quickly, too hard, and should say, instead, that I will do all in *my* power to rid these weapons from our midst. I know folks on all sides of the so-called "right-to-bear-arms" debate, and I grew up in a hunting culture myself. So I am not talking about the spheres of law-abiding citizens who themselves would oppose paranoid, right-wing zealots. But I do not think it is too much to ask that we do all in our power to discuss and then enact the elimination of these sorts of weapons. Yes, it has

been illegal to sell such weapons since 1994, but I would suggest something further, a buy-back program to get these instruments of death completely off the streets and away, not just from distressed and despairing teenagers but from all people everywhere.)

(5) **We will take care of the earth.** We will preserve and conserve the earth for our youth and their future. We understand that a sustainable and sustaining earth is a great bequest to you, and we pledge ourselves to knowing with all of our hearts and minds and souls that "the earth is the Lord's and the fullness thereof," and therefore whenever we squander or misuse the earth, we are not only profaning a great gift from God but we are robbing our children and youth from their full inheritance. We will take care of the earth.

(6) **We will provide you with the knowledge you need.** Obviously, knowledge is required for a fulfilling life of work and play and growth. This congregation this day recommits its membership to doing what we have done for the past two years: providing a $1,000 scholarship for every Community youth who graduates from high school or its equivalent. We will also provide tutoring, guidance, and other supportive services for youth who desire them.

(7) **We will inspire you with the wisdom we have received.** Wisdom is absolutely needed for a meaningful life of maturing grace. With the inherited wisdom from elders we have made our way – not only with sufficiency but success in the best sense of the word. And we hope and pray to impart such wisdom onto you.

(8) **We will model for you a reverence for God.** In other words, we will not be timid about our concerns about ultimate matters. We will share our belief in God and our faith

through Christ. We will show forth our beliefs–given flesh in the regular practices of our faith–in the Creator of the universe, who offers the gift of Jesus Christ as Savior, and who sustains us through the presence of the Holy Spirit in an ongoing reality in and through the Church. No longer will it be acceptable for us to "drop off the kids" for Sunday School and worship and take in breakfast at Winstead's or First Watch or elsewhere, and then pick up the kids afterwards. We will sit with you in class and in worship and then share with you what we have experienced together.

(9) **We will love your parents.** In fact it may be as important to love your parents as it is to love you. For we have been grasped by the searing truth: "Hungry parents cannot feed children." As we love your parents–through caring attention, through supportive education events, through providing counsel, guidance and affirmation for them in their crucial roles–we also love you.

(10) **We will foster healthy ways and means in which you can rebel.** We know that part of the maturing process for youth is establishing their own paths of fashion, music, style and personal expression in the world. And we confess that adults have sometimes been far too focused on what body parts some youth are piercing than what issues are piercing their souls. But we too have known rebellion. We too know what it once was to want to wear clothes and hair in certain ways, much to the consternation of parental authorities. We will do our part to be sensitive to need to rebel. But we will furthermore do whatever it takes to provide healthy contexts in which you can express your personal inclinations as youth.

Such are the "Five Proposals for Parents" and "Ten Commitments to Youth" by the Church, which can empower us to live out the challenging word for the Lord–"Do not be overcome by evil." The last word in this declaration really belongs to the youth and people of Littleton, Colorado, however. In their own words–in a song created for a mass memorial service just a week ago–they have issued an invitation to us all.

Columbine, Flower Blue, Tenderly, I sing to you.

Columbine, Rose, Blood-Red, but Heartbreak overflows my head.

Columbine, Flower Blue, Columbine, there's hope for you.

Columbine, Friend of Mine

Turn our pain...to your gain. Keep our heart...on the mark.

Comfort us with your love, Love again.

Columbine, Friend of Mine.

Our response to that invitation is, at least in part, this message though there be those who have been crushed by the current crisis, yet they and we have hope because Christ is in their midst. We will do all that we can, with the grace of God, to "turn their pain...to everyone's gain, to keep their and our hearts on the mark, to comfort them with love, so that they might love again." Perhaps we begin to overcome evil with good in powerful, reconciling wondrous ways by saying, "Columbine, Friend of Mine." AMEN.

Notes

1 e-mail from Mike Hays, pastor of Britton Christian Church, Oklahoma City, Oklahoma

5

Overcoming the Church's Biggest Crisis

Text: Acts 1:15-26

It would be easy to embroil ourselves in an endless debate over which *"latest crisis"* is the greatest for us this morning. The specter of war, of course and naturally, looms large on the horizon of our national landscape and the world stage. Economic pressure and instability–played out in real lives among folks who suffer real lay-offs and know real financial anxieties–could easily preoccupy us for the entire morning.

And some of you have indicated to me in no less than seven e-mails this week recently that the real crisis is the confusion we all face in the world of communication. To wit, we regularly do not and maybe cannot get it right when it comes to speaking and listening and exchanging proper bits of information. In a time in history when the amount of the world storebank of knowledge is doubling nearly every three-four years, we are ever feeble and fallible creatures when it comes to communicating that knowledge.

For Christians, however, the most exacting crisis, the real

"cruncher" for the Church, has to do with something more pressing even than layoffs, something more challenging than proper communication, and something more lastingly important than currently averting international conflict.

Properly stated our biggest crisis this morning as Christians is the same crisis that faced the early church just after Jesus' resurrection and his ascension. To put a one-word name on that crisis, let's use the word "LEADERSHIP."

"Who will lead us?" goes the cry from nearly every quarter in nearly every Christian denomination. In some mainline denominations like our own, the Christian Church (Disciples of Christ), the crisis is acute. It is estimated by our own Pension Fund leaders that nearly half of all current Disciples clergy among our churches will retire, die, or otherwise discontinue their full-time service by the year 2020. "Who will lead us?" we ask with urgency and fervent worry.

"The search is not going well," says the head of one pulpit search committee after another in a litany of testimonies by one congregation after another facing a pool of candidates that is not as deep and wide as it once was. "Who will lead us?" the question persists.

Rocked by the lack of priests and religious to lead them and the bruising of publicly aired and rancorous scandal, the Roman Catholic Church combines parishes and closes churches nearly every week. "Who will lead us?" is also a refrain among our Catholic brothers and sisters.

It is very important to note that just three months ago, the Rev. Dr. Richard Hamm submitted his resignation as our General Minister and President, effective at the end of the forthcoming General Assembly in Charlotte, North Carolina, two years prior to the normal ending of his term. "Who will lead us?" we ponder, again, on all levels of this denomination in which we hold dear and now tested loyalties.

Well, please see with me that we are not without precedent in this leadership crisis. More pointedly, we can see from our text this morning that ours isn't as bad a situation as the early Church faced. Consider the early Church's challenges as we find them at the outset of the book of Acts. Leadership was obviously its number one problem. After the resurrection, after the ascension, the Church has a premier set of problems. Please note what they are up against:

- trying either to be safe or get out of Jerusalem alive;
- pondering what the revolution of the resurrection was all about and how it would really impact their lives;
- tending to the hole in their physical reality – the master, the Savior, the one that the book of Hebrews calls "our Leader," Jesus, is gone;

And, not the least of their challenges:

- picking a replacement for Judas.

You want a problem, here it is: ***leadership!*** But go on and read through the rest of the first portions of the book of Acts and you soon discover that some amazing things happened.

- Spirit comes upon the disciples and other followers of Christ.
- Peter preaches the greatest recorded sermon of his entire preaching career.
- 3000 come to faith at Pentecost.
- And they're off to the races. "I have no silver or gold, but what I have I give you; in the name of Jesus Christ of Nazareth, stand up and walk,"[1] says Peter and people are healed and helped and granted hope left and right.
- Stephen serves as the church's first courageous martyr.
- Saul, one of the greatest persecutors of the early Church, is converted and transformed into Paul, one of its greatest

evangelists.

First the leadership crisis and then–boom!–all this power, and plenty of leaders.

But first, we should repeat, there was a leadership crisis. It is the early Church's biggest crisis. After Jesus is resurrected, after he sends them to Jerusalem to await empowerment, after he leaves the apostles to ponder the disruptive meanings of the gospel as they behold the contrails of his ascension, the question remains: "Who will lead us?" Leadership is the early Church's biggest crisis. Our text shows what is done and the spirit in which it is done to overcome this crisis.

There will be other choices to be made regarding leadership roles in the early church, but this is the first. This particular text simply (and straightforwardly) references the need to fulfill the place left empty by Judas' death and departure from the original circle of the twelve apostles. For Luke there is a need for the re-establishment of the full complement of twelve apostles, partly in alignment with the dream of the apostles leading the twelve tribes of Israel and most assuredly with what Peter (and Luke) believe about the overarching purposes of God.

Our text contains Peter's very first speech, which, while not exactly a sermon, may still be considered his first testimony of faith after Jesus' physical departure from the midst of the disciples. How unafraid he is to face the truth of Judas' betrayal and death. Perhaps because he knows of his own past apostasy, and Christ's forgiving response to his betrayal, even as he speaks. This is daring leadership indeed!

So, note with me what happens in the midst of the early Church's biggest crisis:

1. Peter literally stands up and figuratively steps out on a limb to note the need for Judas's replacement.
2. Peter proffers the criteria by which the new apostle should

be chosen: a person who has "accompanied [the other apostles] during all the time that the Lord Jesus went in and among us," beginning at the inaugural baptism moment at the River Jordan until the time of Jesus' ascension.

3. Peter describes the role and responsibility of the new leader-to-be: "a witness with us to [Jesus'] resurrection."
4. The band of approximately 120 believers chooses two candidates.
5. The believers pray for God's revelation as to who to choose for "this ministry."
6. And they opt for the most mundane and seemingly fair method for their ultimate choice–they cast lots.

And the rest, as we say, is history.

Is that enough to show us how to overcome a leadership crisis in the Church? Are the early Church's experiences and examples sufficient? Do we have an answer to our own question: "Who will lead us?"

We can say that the process through which Peter led the first circle of Jesus' followers did in fact work for them. Once the leadership vacuum had been filled, empowerment erupted. From our contemporary perspective 2000 years after the fact, the choice of Matthias doesn't seem to be a "make-or-break" decision, but it set the Church in motion. From what we can discern from our text, Matthias' credentials had mostly to do with proximity to the apostle's inner circle and not a powerful personality. His resume is never really revealed but his addition to the apostles has less to do with his capability and more to do with his availability. And all along Peter and the rest of the remnant of Jesus' followers after his ascension seem to be trusting in God to do something mighty with their efforts.

In the face of our own leadership crises, I wonder if we make way too much of our daunting dilemmas and troublesome times. I wonder if it might be enough, really might be sufficient, if we employed a strategy similar to Peter's and did something like the following:

7. Let us stand up and state the emphatic case for replacements in the church's leadership ranks. Someone "***must become*** a witness with us to his resurrection."
8. Let us recruit among ourselves those who have gifts for ministry by virtue of their close proximity to the Church's activities. While Jesus' physical presence and historical ministry is now 2,000 years old, his body, the Church, is the locale for recruitment future leaders. And in this regard, let current pastors, ministers, elders, and diaconate members abound in our affirmations and inquiries among potential candidates for ministry. When was the last time you asked someone, "Have you ever thought of the vocation of ministry for your life's work?"
9. And let us then pray for God's guidance all along the way, trusting that the power he promised to deliver to the first Church – "But you shall receive power..."[2] – will happen to us as a new and renewing Pentecost moment.

Sound impossible? Sound way too grandly idealistic? Sound too unwieldy and unpredictable? Is the leadership crisis more than we can handle? Well of course it is, if we depend solely on our own powers and wherewithal. Peter knew that and we know that too. But Peter and the early Church knew and trusted something else too. They knew the wisdom and saving truth of an old adage that goes like this: "You know something is of God, if it's big and it's beautiful and it's impossible!" Let us know this wisdom and claim this truth for our time!

Notes
1 Acts 3:6
2 Acts 1:8

6

Peace and the Prophet's Heart

20th Annual World Peace Meditation – An Interfaith Peace Gathering, Rime Buddhist Center, Kansas City, Missouri

Good morning! Blessings on everyone who is here. Blessings on everyone who is awake. And a double portion of abundant blessings on the sacred ones among us who can claim membership in both of those groups.

But not only *"Good Morning"* and "Blessings," but, more importantly, *"Peace!"* And also, *"La Paz," "Mir," "Salaam," "Shalom," "Shanti," "Ereine."* Yes, especially this day, *"Peace!"*

I'm honored and humbled by the invitation to proffer some remarks this august morning on the back side of the back side of the passing year and the dawning of a new one. And on the occasion of the 20th anniversary of this sacred meeting.

I'm honored and humbled by the task at hand – the praying in and breaking in and welcoming in of Peace. I'm honored because there is no greater cause for citizens of the world. I'm humbled because of the daunting nature of the task.

Allow me, if you will, for just a few moments, to say what

I believe is a crucial connection between *"Peace and the Prophet's Heart."* For if we are about peace, it is surely a prophetic task. And if we take seriously the prophetic calling on the cusp of a new year, we cannot help but focus on peace.

It has seemed to me of late that a prophet's heart is a distinctly beautiful, four-chambered organ.

One chamber is for righteous anger in the face of gross injustice.

Rather than an emotion to be avoided at all costs, anger is always one of the purest and most appropriate responses to a violated value. For example:

- Anger—at our disregard of the earth.
- Anger at the abuse of children.
- Anger when we are in the situation which Sister Corita describes from her perch at Operation Breakthrough in the heart of the heart of Kansas City: *"How strange that we collect aluminum cans and yet throw away children."*
- Anger at our ceaseless clutching after things and more things when we already have so much—too much!? (Maurice Sendak is really right, isn't he, when he says *"There must be something more to life than just having everything."*)
- Anger over the disallowance of freedom wherever people yearn to be free.
- Anger because the earth is soaked in the blood of war and the winds are choking with the stench of disease and the rivers are fouled by indifference.
- Anger at the idiotic irony that there is enough food for all people, but not enough political will to see that the food gets to the people.

Yes, anger is one chamber in the four-chambered organ of the Prophet's Heart.

And there is also one chamber for compassion to the

point of sorrow in the face of unthinking cruelty and (even worse) willful, mendacious, snaky evil. Of all the virtues the prophets embody in the Hebrew scriptures – including especially Isaiah, Jeremiah, Amos, Hosea, and Micah – compassion is the premier, signal characteristic.

Richard Lischer has recently identified this key characteristic of the prophets for me in his new book *The End of Words*. He says we too often stereotype the prophets' dominant tone as that of anger. But Lischer says "No," the dominant tone of the prophets is not anger but sorrow.

We could do with a lot more compassion to the point of sorrow:

- Compassion for the ones blinded by ambition and blindered by provincial perspectives.
- Compassion for the most vulnerable. (We all know the "seventh law of thermo-spiritual dynamics," even at 6:00 o'clock in the morning: *Parents always play favorites among children; a mother or father always loves most the child that needs them the most at a given moment.)*
- And compassion to the point of sorrow even for those who succumb to stupidity like xenophobia, or the cynicism that leads to despair, or the hurt that leads to hate and even greater hate. Compassion even for ones like Fred Phelps.

And then there is one chamber for ecstatic joy in the presence of holiness and the triumph of truth. Peacemakers always have an impish joy in them, don't they? Consider: the Dali Llama, or Thomas Merton, or Will Campbell, or William Sloane Coffin, or Dorothy Day, or Lama Chuck Stanford.

Yes, joy in the presence of holiness, holiness like arising early enough this morning to be here by 6:00 am for a worship service in an interfaith gathering.

- Holiness like fresh, warm bread broken and blessed by the

words, *"Baruch atah Adonai, Eloheinu..."*

- Holiness like a wise child who laughs out loud because the king has no clothes on.
- Holiness like Mohandas K. Gandhi possessed when he said, "*When I despair, I remember that all through history the way of truth and love has always won. Oh, there have been tyrants and murderers and for a time than can seem to prevail. But in the end they always fall. Think of it. Always.*" And I believe he said that somber sounding phrase with a bit of an impish grin.

I treasure the definition of peace that Rev. Veronica Goines provided for her congregation at St. Andrew Presbyterian Church in Marin City, California, "Peace is joy at rest, and joy is peace on its feet."

Finally one chamber in the prophet's heart is always reserved for hope. Always hope. Hope is and always must be the fourth and final chamber of the prophet's heart.

- Hope is the dynamo at the center of peacemaking that drives the engine of activism.
- Hope is the kernel of every faith worthy of the name.
- Hope is what moves us forward and raises babies above the flood-waters and shines a piercing light into the reckless rubble rendered by the too-quick earthquake.
- Hope, the motivation for every person who wants children to grow, cultures to prosper, music to be magnified, and truth to triumph.
- Hope, that innate given, that incessant impetus for the beating of the heart, your heart, my heart, every heart, and the reason we will continue praying and meditating for peace until the cows of Bashan come home and the way of war grounds down into silent uselessness and every person inherits the possibility of experiencing their tremendous ca-

pacities for beauty and attainment and grace and love.

Yes, remember today the connection between peace and the four-chambered capacity of a prophet's heart:

- One chamber for righteous anger in the face of injustice;
- One chamber for compassion to the point of sorrow, in the face of unthinking cruelty or (even worse) willful, mendacious snaky evil;
- One chamber for ecstatic joy in the presence of holiness and the triumph of truth; and
- One chamber for hope, always hope.

And when our hearts beat in rhythm with one another, we will see that day come 'round when peace will be at the heart of the world and anger will dissolve and compassion will be everything and joy will color the skies and hope will be fulfilled.

So, again, "Good Morning," "Blessings," and "Peace" upon all of our little prophetic, four-chambered hearts. May there be abundant improvement in our cardiac care in the new year. Amen and may God bless you. And...Peace!

7

What Then Shall We Say

(The Five Things a Minister Has to Say)

Text: Romans 8:31

On the Occasion of the Ordination of
The Rev. Kimi Yokoyama Whipple

Word of Thanks–

Before we proceed any further, let's be honest about our hopes and dreams about the minister we hope and trust will come to the fore in our denomination.

We have some parameters of hope. We have some assumed profiles of what is needed. We'd like our ministers to aspire to certain ideals. We'd like our ministers, especially our newest ministers, to be...

as daring as Deborah;
as faithful as Ruth;
as untiring as Moses;
as wise as Solomon;
as close to The Master as Mary Magdalene;
as loyal to Jesus as his own mother;

as biblically savvy as Marcus Borg;
as homiletically profound as Fred Craddock;
as passionate in her leadership as Cynthia Hale;
as focussed on purpose as Rick Warren;
as sensitive to seekers as Bill Hybels;
as full of courageous wit as Bill Coffin;
as prophetic as Will Campbell;
as engaged with evangelicals as Tony Campolo;
as with-it in worship as Sally Morgenthaler;
as relationally connected with others as Paul Diehl;
as good with appliances as the Maytag Man;
as skilled on a computer as Bill Gates;
as good in the kitchen as Emeril;
as popular as Oprah;
as impressive on the putting green as Michele Wie;
as long off the tee as Tiger Woods;
and as good in the yodeling department as Barbara Oldham.

We'd prefer our ministers to be...

In Shape–but not so much so that they make us hyper aware of own lack in that category;

Up-to-date–but not so far out in front of their people that their people mistake them for the enemy;

Top Rate–but not so good that they incite feelings of inferiority among their colleagues;

Down to Earth–but not so much that we think they're merely "dirty;"

Heavenly Minded–but not so much that they can't do any earthly good.

Yes, we want great ministers!

This afternoon, I want to lift up a pinnacle moment in the correspondence of the apostle Paul for our mutual consideration.

I refer, of course to the book of Romans–

- the *"Matterhorn"* of Paul's highest theology,
- the *"Grand Canyon"* of his deepest convictions,
- the Ultimate Equation for Equity between the sky of the gospel's promise and the earthen reality of the gospel being lived out.[1]

Most specifically, I mean this morning to lift up the 31st verse of the 8th chapter. You may have missed it, regarding it as a merely conjunctive phrase, a rhetorical question in no need of an answer. But I want to lift up the 31st verse as a "working project" question–as Howard Thurman might put it–as the thematic emphasis that the apostle Paul would have us all address as people of God, and especially for pastors who lead the people of God.

What I'm suggesting is that Paul's seemingly innocent question is the very center of his concerns at this time as the chief missionary of the Church. This question is the very essence of what needs to be considered for a pastor and a people, and a church that wants to make a significant difference in the 21st century.

"What then shall we say...?"

It seems to me that there are, straightforwardly speaking, a literal handful of things any minister has within their capacity to say as pastor of a congregation or in any other ministerial position. And the first of these things is:

I. "Hello!"

To say "Hello!" is to proffer an attitude of welcoming grace to others. To say "Hello!"is to refuse to treat others, as they are too often treated each and every day, as invisible. To say "Hello!" is to recognize the deep indwelling of both humanity and divinity in each and every heart we encounter.

Sometimes all a minister needs to do to create a space for

grace–in an individual's life or within the fellowship of a congregation–is merely to say "Hello!" That and leading others to say "Hello!" to one another. I'm convinced that 100% of half of the world's problems is because we have not properly, caringly, carefully enough met each other. In those instances, someone forgot to say "Hello!"

Ministers are to say "Hello!" to a lot of folks and to introduce them to the practice of saying "Hello!" To say "Hello!" to one another. To say "Hello!" to their best selves. To lead church members to say "Hello!" to the wider community, particularly those yet without a church home. To lead congregations and other churchly institutions to embodying a sense of "Hello!" and thereby showing the world that there are persons and institutions that care.

We abide in a world too often numbed by anonymity, immobilized by indifference, and desperately waiting for someone, to say, as John Prine puts it, "Hello in there!" When you do so, you perform every-day miracles. And it is a blessed event to behold.

II. I Love You!

I hardly need to remind anyone here that beyond every Christian theology and beneath every assumption of the Christian faith, love is the essence of what it means to follow Jesus. However, I may need to remind you ***to say*** the words "I love you!"

Of all the utterances needing more frequent citation in the official transcripts of Church life, the phrase "I love you!" has to be near the top of the list.

Saying "I love you!" with our lips and with our lives.

Saying "I love you!" like the early Church did: *"And they devoted themselves to the apostles teaching and fellowship, to the breaking of bread and the prayers."*[2]

How could this blueprint for the Church's life and witness have become so real, so vibrant? Only with love, and with the fellowship as a whole saying, with sincerity and genuineness, "I love you!"

Despite the fact that his thought set the whole modern way of being human into motion, the philosopher Descartes really had it wrong. "*Cogito ergo sum,*" he posited. "I think, therefore I am." Oh, no! It really is, "*Amo, ergo sum.*" "I love, therefore I am."[3]

Raymond Carver, of great short story and poetry fame, knew intimately that love and saying "I love you!" were at the heart of any fruitful human enterprise. In one of his most memorable poems, he says:

And did you get what
you wanted from this life, even so?
I did.
And what did you want?
To call myself beloved, to feel myself
beloved on the earth.[4]

III. "What's going on?"

This is the third thing a minister has the capacity to say. When we are at the side of one in a hospital bed offering prayer, when we are talking things over after a project has concluded, when we are hanging out at coffee fellowship, we're basically asking a simple, yet sometimes revolutionary question: "What's going on?"

When we're teaching a Bible study class, and someone comes from left field with one of those bombshell queries, they're exercising the right they share in sacred mutuality with you to ask "What's going on?"

"What's going on..." with this text, with this line of theology, or with that particular tradition?

The Church needs a whole lot more people asking "What's going on?" We are in need of fresh, newly energized leaders, who are unafraid and unvanquished in their quest for more and better light.

To ask "What's going on?" is the first step in bringing dreams into focus and then the focussed dreams into reality.

To ask "What's going on?" may be the most liberating thing any pastor asks when they are first coming on board and assuming their duties. This is not mere fact-finding. Rather, it is the establishment of the freedom (and the responsibility) to ask important questions about some of the most important issues in a person's or an institution's life.

IV. "Good"

In a way we all need to be "Barnabas," who embodied his name, which means "son of encouragement." We are more in need of this word than many realize. In an atmosphere suffocating with cut-throat rhetoric and a generic spirit of acrimony, in an overly long moment in history when "what bleeds leads," in a culture which is addicted to the salacious, the seamy, and the grotesque, we need a positive word of grace. I nominate the word "Good" for such a role.

This is the word which, if we would pronounce it more often, would help us live out the *imago dei* in which we were born. May we never forget that, according to Genesis' creation drama, the first word recorded as coming out of God's mouth, after "let there be...," was "Good!" And then "Very good!"

Too many Christians, walk around presuming badness, acting as if they had been baptized in vinegar laced with garlic. I wonder if they have forgotten Paul's great conviction? ***"Who shall separate us from the love of Christ? Shall tribulation, or distress, or persecution, or famine, or nakedness, or peril, or sword?...No, in all these things we are more than conquerors*** *through him who loved us. For I am sure that neither death, nor life, nor angels, nor principalities, nor things present, nor things to come, nor powers, nor height, nor depth, nor anything else in all creation, will be able to separate us from the love of God in Christ Jesus our Lord."* And if we believe that is true then what better word for us to pronounce upon a people or a place than "Good"!!??

This relates to a strategy for doing ministry in the world, too. Too often ministers become shackled by the tyranny of negativism in a particular culture. Too often we fall prey to the influence of the "boo-birds" who degrade the Church's importance or disregard the gospel's relevancy. Ordination is sometimes like an infatuating flame to the those moths who live life in the minus column.

They are the ones who shout "No!" in the face of any possibility of change.

They are the ones who vote "No!" on the question of whether the Church can ever impact the world with goodness.

In the face of these nay-saying *"nudnicks,"* to use a good Yiddish phrase, be sure, people of God, to "Count the 'Yes' votes!"[5]

"Counting the 'Yes' votes is the only thing that has ever moved the world forward and liberated the oppressed and healed the sick and offered hope to folks weighed down in the swamps of negativism.

And if you, if we all, are persistent enough, I'm convinced that not only is the apostle Paul right, once more, that nothing can separate us from the love of God. I'm also sure that the sour notes of the "boo-birds" can be – will be! – transformed into a chorus of "Hallelujahs!"

V. "Good-bye"

Of course the fifth thing a minister has the capacity to say is "Good-bye." Now, I don't mean simply at the conclusion of a ministry or the finishing of a task with a particular congregation.

Instead, I'm emphasizing that you and all ordained clergy leaders are in the business of helping others say "Good-bye."

"Good-bye"–so long–to unholy habits.

"Good-bye"–so long–to defeats.

"Good-bye"–so long–to outmoded ways of being.

"Good-bye"–so long–to childish ways that no longer help us become the children of God.

"Good-bye"–so long–to old-fogey-ism that hinders us from becoming truly mature in Christ.

"Good-bye"–so long.

As all the ministers present here this afternoon do, as all Christians do, too, as you help others say their good-byes to those they love the most. These are indeed the most "teachable moments" in ministry. That has been my experience and that of countless others who have served as you are about to serve.

This isn't another form of saying "so long." This is a far richer and much deeper experience than that.

The original form and meaning of the word "Good-bye" is "God...be...with...ye." "God be with you." In other words, it's a benediction, a blessing, a good word for going, a word for sending forth. This is what the apostle Paul does at the end of Romans, with all those names and all those greetings. What is he saying? As important as anything else he had written to them up to that point. "Good-bye" "God be with you."

So, to answer the question which Paul asks of the Romans and of his successors, and especially of ordained ministers, "What then shall we say?" it would seem to me that these five things are a good place to start. They are, at the very least, five of the things which any minister worth his or her salt has the capacity to say:

"Hello!"

"I love you!"

"What's going on?"

"Good!"

"Good-bye."

And if a minister says these five things among the countless other things he or she says in a lifetime of service to fulfill his or her ordination, then they will have said a mouthful, indeed a life-full. And that not only will do. That will do just fine. AMEN.

Notes

1 The metaphorical turn here is originally Fred Craddock's.

2 Acts 2:42

3 This insight is originally William Sloane Coffin's.

4 Raymond Carver, "Late Fragment," *A New Path to the Waterfall* (NY: Atlantic Monthly Press, 1989), p. 122.

5 Lyle Schaller first coined this phrase.

8

A Way Out of No Way

Text: John 1:43-51

My strong and sincere thanks to Joanne Verburg for the initial invitation to be here the 20th Anniversary Celebration of Covenant Christian Church and for the excellent hospitality that's been laid out so generously since I arrived. She is a sterling colleague and in her you have a true treasure here in your congregation. You are blessed to an overwhelming measure, I believe, to have two clergy like Joanne and Anna Perry as your pastoral leaders. Joanne, I have come to know over the years and Anna I have recently met through the Bethany Fellows project. With clergy like these your future is bright indeed.

And what can I say but an embarrassed word of gratitude for the extraordinary graces that have been extended to me by Don and Shirley Lucey. I am just finding out what you all (and countless ones across the face of our denomination) have known forever: it is an absolute treasure to be in their company.

And to Jimmy Mohler, Community member *extraordinaire*,

let me to say I am delighted to see you. And I would echo the words of Psalm 139 and also say, "Whither shall I go from thy Spirit? Whither shall I flee from thy presence? If I ascend up into the heavenly pulpit of Community Christian Church, thou art there. If I make my place in Washington, D.C., thou art there. If I take the wings of the morning and dwell in the uttermost locale of Covenant Christian Church in Cary, North Carolina, even there thy hand shall greet me and thy countenance shall meet me!"

Søren Kierkegaard tells a parable of a community of ducks waddling off to duck church to hear the duck preacher. The duck preacher spoke eloquently of how God had given the ducks wings with which to fly. With these wings there was nowhere the ducks could not go, there was no God-given task the ducks could not accomplish. With those wings they could soar into the presence of God himself. Shouts of "Amen" were quacked throughout the duck congregation. At the conclusion of the service, the ducks left, commenting on what a wonderful message they had heard–and waddled all the way back home. May such a fate for us be avoided here at Covenant Christian Church, in Cary, North Carolina, this morning!

Our text for the morning is one of the most stirring and inspiring sections of John's gospel. The scene is exciting, the situation is urgent. This is John's telling of the beginning of Jesus' gathering of his disciples for the work of his ministry. John has moved deftly (and with a master theologian's touch) from the beautifully abstract poetry of his *Logos* prolegomenon –*"In the beginning was the word and the word was with God and the word was God"*–to the concrete reality and ultimacy of Jesus' calling of the twelve. Jesus' calling of the disciples follows quickly on the heels of John the Baptist's ministry and his prophetic proclamation of Jesus' processional. Jesus calls first Andrew, then Peter (and in the process of giving him a new direction for his life, he also gives him a new destiny by virtue of a new name).

Then Jesus turns his attention away. *Away* from Bethany from whence he had just come and *away* from Jerusalem, from which they were already sending out emissaries from the *"Judean National Inquirer"*–their motto (*"Inquiring minds want to know"*) hasn't changed in 2000 years!!–and *away* from the fishing nets at Bethsaida where Peter and Andrew had left them drying in the sun. Now Jesus shifts his visual gaze and his walking gate toward Galilee. There he finds Philip. Immediately he discerns that he wants Philip in the movement and challenges him: "Follow me." Then the dynamics of the story shift in a dramatic manner.

Cynthia Ozick says there are basically two archetypes of stories which can be described by simple summary phrases: (1) *"A stranger came to town."* and (2) *"We were on a journey."* In this scene from John's gospel, we have both–a confluence of both types: Jesus, a stranger to most up to this point in the story, has come to town; and now the newly developed disciples' "dream team" is commencing on a journey. And into this confluence comes nettlesome, nagging, nay-saying Nathaniel.

For too long we have been too kind to Nathaniel. We've let him off the hook. Let us look at what the Bible says that he says and does, and thus learn from him.

I. The First "No Way!"

Nathaniel's main retort to Philip's entreaty concerning Jesus being the Messiah is "No way!" Oh, he puts it politely enough in the form of a question: *"Can anything good come out of Nazareth?"* But it's really a rhetorical question! Nathaniel says, in effect, ***"There's no way that anything good can come out of Nazareth."*** His is the expression of provincial prejudice and uninspired misinformation. Sometimes this sort of sentiment is expressed in our own lives, within the context of our own venues:

Can anything good come out of...Kansas City, Missouri?

Can anything good come out of...Raleigh, North Carolina?

Can anything good come out of...Ohio State?

Can anything good come out of...The Carolina Panthers?

Can anything good come out of...The Kansas City Royals?

Can anything good come out of...a youth with a pierced __?

Can anything good come out of...of a person with gray hair?

Can anything good come out of...the mainline churches?

Can anything good come out of...a small congregation?

Can anything good come out of...a large congregation?

Can anything good come out of...the evangelical churches?

Can anything good come out of...the Disciples of Christ?

And when we participate in any portion of that litany, we are echoing Nathaniel's cynical sentiment: *"No way!"* To which Philip politely and simply replies: "Come and see." Not coercion, but invitation to a new way of seeing.

Sometimes others help us see in new ways. A member of Community, Dorothy Hughart, was once "Philip" to my "Nathaniel" within Community's family of faith. She had invited me to her house to visit. She said she had some family pictures to share with me. Whoopee! I thought. I got to her door which she flung open with gladness and glee. Ushering me into her living room, she quickly set me down on the sofa and proceeded with pleasantries and a recounting of her entire family history. Then she pulled out a little red wagon loaded with picture albums which we leafed through and leafed through and leafed through. For two hours! (I began trying to remember if

Dante's *Inferno* had included a rung of torture called "viewing family albums.")

Then Dorothy said to me: "I saved the very best for last." She tenderly drew out of her front dress pocket a single photograph. "This is a picture of my newest grandson, David, beautiful, beautiful David. He's eight months old in this picture. He's just gorgeous isn't he?" When I received it from her cradling hand, I noticed that the photo depicted the countenance of a child with a cleft palate–the most acutely split lip I had ever seen. "But...," I began to say to Dorothy. And she leaned toward me with eagerness. "Do you see? Isn't he beautiful? Isn't he gorgeous?" I hadn't really seen. I was ready to say, "No way." Yet, Dorothy showed me and, in essence, said, "Come and see." And by her kind invitation, I began to see and through new, tear-glistened eyes I did see. "Yes, David was and is absolutely beautiful!"

II. The Second "No Way!"

Despite his hesitancy, Nathaniel ventures to see for himself. But before he can open his mouth with a greeting, Jesus enunciates one of the most complimentary salutations in the history of greetings: "Behold, and Israelite in whom there is no guile." No deceit, Jesus is saying, not a smidgen of speaking or acting in a clandestine, underhanded way. But, again, Nathaniel resists and in effect, declares ***"No Way!"*** *'Where did you get to know me?"* In essence, Nathaniel is declaring, ***"There is no way that you could know me!"***

Jesus has not yet met Nathaniel; this is unusual! Normally, a salutation of such grand affirmation comes at the conclusion of a long-standing relationship or when summarizing the end of a long and full life. Such as when Einstein considered the meaning of Gandhi's life just after the great Mahatma had died: "Generations to come will scarce believe that such a one as this ever in flesh and blood walked upon this earth."

Is Jesus pronouncing a final benediction on Nathaniel whom he hardly knows? No. Jesus knows something about Nathaniel's "best self," simply by observing him. Nathaniel and Philip and the rest of the called disciples are not the only ones who have decided to come and see. Jesus is doing some seeing of his own! Jesus sees Nathaniel better than Nathaniel can see himself. Jesus sees that Nathaniel is truly an embodiment of the meaning of his very name: "gift of God."

It always takes others to see us as we truly are. Take "John" one of our teenagers at Community. For quite some time, "John" had always thought himself a loser, from the wrong side of the tracks, part of what some folks in certain parts of the United States call "poor white trash." "John" is poor to be sure, inarticulate for the most part (until recently), and a resident in a dingy and dirty trailer park. "John" once was quite sullen, depressed looking. Until he met and started hanging around Jewel Hogan, one of Community's stellar elders. Now "John" has a zip in his step, and almost a sparkle in his eye, and surely a liveliness to his life that was never there before. All because he has suddenly recognized the great inheritance of faith he has form his friends in his church family and especially from the one who is like his second father. Jewel Hogan. While it really should not matter, one of the more interesting aspects of the friendship which "John" and Jewel share is the fact that Jewel is African-American and "John" is Anglo. Such is the power of the gospel; such is the legacy of Christian belief. Because of Jewel's great bequest of faith and love and caring for this teenager, "John" knows some new realities about himself and his future: he knows he's still poor, and he's quite aware that he's white; but he's not trash anymore.

III. The Third "No Way!"

Then, suddenly, Nathaniel realizes that this special teacher who can see so clearly into his life is as Philip said he was when he first encountered him: This one is the Christ. *"Rabbi, you are the Son of God! You are the King of Israel!"* Nathaniel exclaims. What is Nathaniel saying? Once more, he's at it again. What Nathaniel is really saying is ***"There's no way it gets any better than this!!"*** According to John's gospel, it's the first declaration of faith in the drama of the disciples with Jesus. This gospel story also shows what Jesus experiences in Nathaniel's declaration. In Nathaniel's great declaration, Jesus hears a negation, and he almost laughs: *"Do you believe because I told you that I saw you under the fig tree? You will see greater things than these."* Or in Missouri vernacular, ***"You believe because I told you I saw you under the fig tree over yonder? You ain't seen nothing yet! You will see greater things than this, for sure!"***

I once thought that I'd had heard all there was to hear and seen all there was to see about the ravishing beauty and spellbinding wonder of Africa. While visiting South Africa in 1988, I thought, "It doesn't get any better than this!" Capetown, the most beautiful city on the face of the earth, for my money. Mfanefile, in KwaZulu, where the stars are so brilliantly bright, like blossoms of light you can pick from the sky. Beholding the beauty of the people, as well as the land. "There's no way," I thought, "it can ever get any better than this!" Then I enjoyed a rare opportunity to go to Cameroon.

On the trip to Cameroon, I was privileged to serve as "spiritual director" for a group of 15 folks, mostly Oklahoma Citians, who had endured and survived the horrors of the bombing of April 19, 1995. The group was called "C.O.U.R.A.G.E." Cameroon, Oklahoma United in Recovery And Growth through Exchange. On our two-week sojourn, I discovered how God can gently, powerfully lead any and all of us out of being stuck in "No Way" life postures.

We trekked to Cameroon, because in the Lake Nyos area, in 1985, a gaseous explosion erupted, killing 1,745 people, sometimes three and four generations of an entire family, and more than 4,500 head of livestock. Into this seemingly despair-soaked rainforest we trekked. We were on a people-to-people exchange in order to learn how the Cameroonians had learned to cope with and perhaps overcome their grief. In turn, there was the clear intention to effect healing in all of our hearts, and to be ambassadors of good will in an experiencing of mutual sharing.

Among the Oklahoma Citians was Mike Lenz. His wife Kathy had been six months pregnant, when on Tuesday night, April 18, 1995, they had gone to the doctors to see a sonogram. It was a boy, the video revealed, and Mike and Kathy were ecstatic. They named the child in the womb: Mike III. Then the next morning, April 19, at 9:02, Kathy was tragically, sorrowfully, included in the 168 casualties—dead, and the baby too.

On the faces, in the postures, infused throughout the conversations, and seemingly in the very air of the C.O.U.R.A.G.E. entourage, there seemed to be a theme: *"There's 'No Way' that we can overcome the bloody nightmares, and the haunting daydreams, and the living hell of loss."*

During our travels through the beautiful landscapes of the West Africa Edenic garden and among the even more beautiful people of Cameroon, the Oklahoma Citians shared with the Cameroonians in "survivor meetings." "What did you do to overcome your grief?" the Oklahoma Citians would ask.

"I drank too much," replied one Cameroonian.

"I did that too," said an Oklahoma Citian.

"I was mean to everybody, including my family, for a long,

long time," said another Cameroonian.

"I did that too," said an Oklahoma Citian.

"I was just crazy for a while, not able to sleep, not able to eat, not able to work, just crazy," remembered one Cameroonian.

"Oh, yeah, been there, done that," sighed an Oklahoma Citian.

Then the survivor group participants heard a Cameroon elder share his perspective. He had walked 15 kilometers–each way–to the village of Bua Bua where we were staying. He was asked, "What did you do to overcome the tragedy at Lake Nyos? How did you get over the sorrow?" He responded very, very straightforwardly, ***"I discovered I had to make a decision whether to give my heart to the dead or to give my heart to the living. I finally chose to give my heart to the living."***

For Mike Lenz, this was a crucial turning point in his life, a turning of a corner in his existence, when he decided that he could indeed get on with the rest of his life: even though he had lost his wife who was pregnant with their son, six months along the way, he was to give his heart to the living. He knew that he needed to give his heart to the living. Mike would say later that when he heard the elder make that statement, he knew he could get on with the rest of his journey as a human being.

CONCLUSION: "A - Way - Out - of - No - Way!"

"No Way!" we say. And we say it with so many different nuances. But with every nuance and in every situation and no matter how we say it, there is a way! There is always "A Way Out of No Way." Now the phrase I've just uttered is from an old, old spiritual. "I know the Lord will make a way, O Yes, he will, he'll make a way out of now way." So let us declare it: *"A - Way - Out - of - No - Way!"*

On this special day of celebration, we know that ***with God there is..."A - Way - Out - of - No - Way!"***

Let us consider. Can anything good come out of the mundane daily experiences of our common life? Oh yes, the magnificent can come out of the mundane, ***because with God there is..."A - Way - Out - of - No - Way!"***

Can anything good come out of 937 E. 22nd Street in Los Angeles, California, in the heart of one of the most challenging neighborhoods in the United States, in the midst of one of the craziest and most discombobulated places on the face of the earth? Oh yes, Saundra Reynolds Bryant can grow up in the nurturing care of a loving home, can mature and learn at All Peoples Christian Center, can achieve her bachelor's degree at Cal Poly, her MSW at the University of Tennessee, and can occupy the Executive Director's seat at the very center which gave her direction, and then be elected First-Vice Moderator of the Christian Church (Disciples of Christ) in the United States and Canada...***because with God there is..."A - Way - Out - of - No - Way!"***

Can anything good come out of Humboldt, Tennessee or Johnson Bible College? Oh yes, indeed, someone can. Fred Craddock can come forth to be the Christian Church's greatest gift to homiletics in the 20th century...***because with God there is..."A - Way - Out - of - No - Way!"***

Can anything good come out of, say, Cary, North Carolina, which starts out as a mere suburb? Oh yes, indeed, something surely can...***because with God there is..."A - Way - Out - of - No - Way!"***

Can anything good come from a small band of Disciples who have a concern—their small building just won't do. Oh yes, indeed, it can, because that small band of Disciples will build this wonderful house of worship for generations yet to come to enjoy...*because with God there is..."A - Way - Out - of - No - Way!"*

Or you may say "No Way" in a different key, with a different inflection. It may be that you think that there's no way it can get any better than a sermon by Joanne Verburg or a sermon by Anna Perry or a program that they create. Whew! "It really doesn't get any better than this!" you might have said on more than one occasion after a stirring worship service, or a fantastic fellowship dinner. And "It'll never get any better than that," you still might be thinking, so full of gladness because of twenty boxes of food provided for the Food Pantry at Urban Ministries and twenty blankets given for Project Linus, and new members like Terry and Katherine White, and Roxie Gold, and Mike Joyce, and Mary Lou Jackson joining this church. But hold on! Along will come another project, another dream, another campaign, another hope-saturated set of events, if you will let them come,...*because with God there is..."A - Way - Out - of - No - Way!"*

Or years from now, you'll be in another space for your 30th or your 40th or your 50th anniversary and then you'll say, "It doesn't get any better than this!" But hold on,...*because with God there is "A - Way - Out - of - No - Way!"*

It may be that some shining Sunday morning, you'll have a worship experience like none other. Easter Sunday morning, or Homecoming Sunday, or Christmas Eve, and your spine is tingling and your soul is soaring and your heart's on fire. And you'll say "There's no way it can get any better than this!" But God will surprise you and later, at the conclusion of a seemingly mundane service, one of your young men or one of your young women will heed the call into ordained ministry, and they'll come forward to make their decision public. And you'll know all over again that *with God there is..."A - Way - Out -*

of - No - Way!"

May we always remember: ***"You will see greater things than these... Very truly, I tell you, you will see heaven opened and the angels of God ascending and descending upon the Son of Man."*** The heart of God and the hearts of humanity opened and love made real, mysterious and magnificent, upon the face of the earth and into the far reaches of heaven, all within the compassionate embrace of Christ, whose life, ministry, crucifixion, death, and resurrection to new life always show us that ***with God there is..."A - Way - Out - of - No - Way!"*** AMEN.

9

One Little Word

Text: Matthew 28:16-20

Introduction

Greetings and thanks once more for the extreme hospitality you've extended to me these past few days. And my how gracious you are to have me speak before you four times in three days. We have had a time, haven't we?!

But given such redundancy and repetition in seeing each other, there may be a few of you who are reciting with me the 19th Psalm:

"I behold you on Sunday morning in the sanctuary and thou art there!, I behold you on Sunday evening in the sanctuary and thou art there. I behold you on Monday evening in the sanctuary and thou art there! And now on Tuesday evening, I behold you once more in the sanctuary and thou art there! Whither shall I go from thy spirit? And whither shall I flee from thy presence?"

So, again, thank you for the wonderful reception and hospitality. And in return for your graciousness, let me assure you, to quote the words of King Henry the 8th to his wife Catherine of Aragon, ***"I won't keep you long."***

One Little Word...

I've brought a word with me today.

It's one of my favorite words.

It's an absolutely essential word for any church's journey now and in the future. It's a good word, and a familiar word to most. The possible candidates for the word I've brought are numerous. The word could be...

Remember – a good word, a precious word, a word that is the mighty engine behind the great propulsion of any holiday observance or special occasion. We've all been doing a lot of remembering these past few days. Remembering our call to discipleship. Remembering Nathaniel and Jesus' challenge to him and us to make "A Way Out of No Way." Remembering. Good word. Excellent word. But I didn't bring that word.

Faith – Could the word be faith? Glad you asked that question. It was very likely the apostle Paul's favorite word. In his magnus opus, the book of Romans he announces clearly: *"For I am not ashamed of the gospel: it is the power of God for salvation to everyone who has faith..."* (Rom. 1:16). And again in Romans he states emphatically, *"Therefore, since we are justified by faith, we have peace with God through our Lord Jesus Christ."* (5:1). "Faith is the substance of things hoped for, the conviction of things not seen," said the writer to the Hebrews (11:1). Faith is the Matterhorn of theology for Paul, a high summit which he hopes to achieve in such a way that he lifts every person along with him as he climbs. Yes, Faith. That would have been a grand and glorious word. But I didn't bring that word.

Hope – "esperanza" in Spanish – a word we need most desperately these days, given the on-going litanies of tragedy in our land and time and in other lands and times. But I didn't bring that word.

Love–the church's most cherished word. While Paul favored the word "Faith" and valued the word "Hope," he would eventually give voice to the most precious word Christians can utter. "So, faith, hope, love, abide, but the greatest of these is love" (1 Cor. 13:13). Yes, that would have been just about the perfect word to bring, wouldn't it. But I didn't bring that word.

Peace–surely this must be the word, since that is what the whole world needs so badly and of which we are in such short supply. As Psalm 122 puts it so simply: *Peace be within your walls. Peace be within you.* But I didn't bring that word.

Used–I could have brought one of my very favorite words, "Used." Marge Piercy has a lovely poem entitled *"To Be of Use."*

Greek amphoras that once held oil,
Hopi vases that held corn, are put in museums
but you know they were made to be used.
The pitcher cries for water to carry
and a person for work that is real.

Yes, "Used" is a good word. But I didn't bring that word.

Today–very first word from Jesus' very first sermon, according to Luke's gospel. But I didn't bring that word.

Hesed–one of my very favorite Hebrew words, whose rough translation in the New Testament comes out to be "grace." But I didn't bring that word.

Good-bye–Money talks I'll not deny, I heard it speak, it said, "Good-bye." Good-bye, meaning ***"God be with you."*** But I didn't bring that word.

Congregation–which is one of the most precious of all words. As one of my preacher friends (with a doctorate no less, a person of great learning and high-minded intelligence) put it last year: "Yes, the theology of the church is important. And yes, the proper hermeneutic of scripture is absolutely necessary for the proper instruction in faith. And yes, of course, a good anthropology is essential if we are to properly and appropriately understand the intersection between the divine and the human. But for most folks, the rubber meets the road at the threshold of the church. Yes, fine and exacting theology and scripture interpretation and the best theories in the world are musts, but, after I learned the words 'God' and 'love' and 'Jesus,' the first holy word I learned was 'congregation.'" But I didn't bring that word.

I could have brought any of the host of words that are awash in the alphabet soup of our shared faith. But today I simply brought one little word from The Great Commission's giant declaration at the conclusion of Matthew's gospel. Maybe you think the word that I've brought this morning is... ***"Make disciples of all nations..."*** There's probably no more important job for the church today than the task of evangelization. And not just bringing people into the church so that you can count the numbers, but disciplining your members, long-standing and those newly entering into fellowship, so that make the numbers count. But I didn't bring that word.

"Baptizing them in the name of the Father, the Son, and the Holy Spirit..." I can tell you this is an important word, perhaps one of the holiest for those of us who are privileged with the task of baptizing new Christians. My friend Will Campbell has a rather distinct and memorable statement about baptizing. He doesn't really have a church much any more, at least not one of the institutional sorts like this one, with four walls, a sign, and all the rest of the appointments that come with such a place and such a people. He does manage to do some counseling and some burying and he writes beautiful books. When he was asked if he ever missed the trappings and blessings of a local church, he said "No." Didn't miss the chance to say, "I now pronounce you husband and wife." Did not miss the affirmation after Sunday services are concluded: "Nice sermon, Rev...." No, what he missed most, he said, was the regular opportunity to say, "In the name of the Father and the Son and the Holy Spirit, I baptize you..." Yes, Baptize. It's a great word. But I didn't bring that word.

"Teaching them to observe all that I have commanded you..." The church was and remains "a house of study." That's a great word: Teaching. There's a Talmudic saying that goes, "An hour in study is like two hours in prayer." Yes, teaching and learning all that Jesus commanded the first disciples and still commands us all about the ways of love, yes, teaching is a great word. But I didn't bring that word.

"And lo, I am with you always..." Trust is the implied imperative here. It's not so much a declared word, but it's certainly part of the meaning of the phrase. That's what I learned – in a new key – from one of my cousins and their abjectly petrified son at our Teague, Texas, family reunion. Amidst about 75 of us on our second cousin James' farm, through tears and bawling moans, he finally heard his father, my cousin, reassure him: "Don't worry. I'm here. I won't leave you. Just follow me." An implied word – Trust. Good word. But I didn't bring that word.

No, the one little word that I've brought here this morning is the word...GO.

Like in Luke 10 – "Go and do likewise."

Like in John 8 – "Go and sin no more."

And here in Matthew 28 – "Go!"

This is the word for the church now!

We ought to sing a new version of "Just as I am..." And instead of ending it with the customary conclusion, "O Lamb of God I come," wouldn't it be better, doesn't the whole world need us to sing "O lamb of God, I...GO?"

This is the word for any and every congregation that wants to be born into a new generation of members and witness for the gospel's sake.

Yes, No, the one little word that I've brought here this evening is the word...*GO.*

So...

Go...Have a dream

Go...Share your dream

Go...into the house of the Lord.

"I was glad when they said unto me, 'Let us GO *into the House of the Lord."*

Before we can ever make disciples, baptize, teach them, or even trust in the Lord's promise of eternal presence with us, we have to "GO!"

While the rest of the world waits at the traffic light of life–and they don't even notice it's a stop sign instead of a stop light!!–the church of Jesus Christ is charged with the high and holy calling to "Go!"

Go–to those in need of the gospel.

Go–to the widow who is hurting yet two years after her beloved died and left his seat at their table saturated with his absence.

Go–to the young person wondering if they really have a place in life.

Go–to the person recuperating from surgery, however major or minor, and go not because you assume you will be Christ to them, but because you are in for the beautiful blessing of them (the least of these, according to Christ's parable in Matthew's gospel) being Christ to you.

Go–to person in jail, whether or not they're a Christian.

Go–to the troubled family, because after all the social agencies have run out of time and money and patience and insurance, the church should be ready with what other non-church groups cannot give: the love of God and the patient acceptance of Christ and the hands of the faithful to help with the healing. Go – Go – Go!

And hear this word especially tonight:

Go – *"Keep going to the evildoers of the World with vigilant and steadfast witness that hate cannot outlast love, and hope shall always prevail over bitterness. Besides, if negativity and hatred and enmity really worked, the world would be a perfect place by now, wouldn't it!?"*

When evil [people] burn and bomb,
good [people] must GO & build and bind.
When evil [people] disrupt and destroy,
good [people] must GO & develop and demonstrate.
When evil [people] hurt and harm,
good [people] must GO & help and heal.
When evil [people] kill,
good [people] must GO & create.
When evil [people] plot,
good [people] must GO & plan.
When evil [people] shout ugly words of hatred,
good [people] must GO and commit themselves to the glories of love.

GO! GO! GO!

One Further Word about Our "One Little Word"

But perhaps you need a new definition of the word go. How about a synonym? I've got one for you. Arising from the verbiage of my Texas roots, surely shared all along the western expanse of the locale wherever the horse became the preeminent mode of transportation, there arose a command that has now traversed cultures and is used anytime one wants to get going. So cowboys and truck drivers, Texans and Missourians alike may use, should use this great word. If "Go" doesn't really suit your fancy, why not "Giddyup!"?

And that's what I came by here this evening to say–Giddyup!

To DeKalb Christian Church–striving to seek God's will and guidance in the new adventures that await you in this momentous year...Giddyup!...Giddyup!

To your pastor Rev. Kent Klundt in all his efforts to provide support and sustenance and healing and hope and inspiration and comfort in his own inimitable way...Giddyup!

To the fellowship groups here–the men and the women and the youth–as you seek new and exciting ways to expand your influence and impact and ministry here in DeKalb and around the world...Giddyup!

To everyone here who yearns to live in that idyllic place as Howard Thurman described it, "a friendly world with friendly kinship underneath friendly skies"...Giddyup!

And now, as I see by my watch, it's time for me to "Go!" Or should I say, "Giddyup!"

10

The Gospel & 'The Passion of the Christ'

Text: II Corinthians 4:13-18

They don't call it "March Madness" for nothing! Welcome to all NAIA fans who are still rooting on their charges. You may just be watching some of the greatest basketball ever, played by heart-strong players, many of them without scholarships and most of them non-NBA possibles, playing only for love of the game and for the honor of their alma mater.

Welcome also to all you expectant, hope-filled, disbelieving KU Jayhawk fans. The Elite Eight is sweet, sweet, sweet, and we'll await with eager anticipation for the next round this afternoon. And a glad and happy welcome to all of you deeply sighing, relieved and jubilant Oklahoma State Cowboy fans! Congratulations on reaching the Final Four. With all the hubbub and vigorous vying for position–not only among teams but among ticket holders!!–it's easy to see how the marketing strategy is very accurate: "March Madness"–indeed!

But there's also another March Madness that's descended upon the whole of the US. This great March Madness could be called Me's "March Madness," given all the excitement generated by his recent movie, *"The Passion of The Christ."*

All the buzz, then fervor, then furor, and finally controversy began a year ago when certain preview groups were asked to field test the movie's script. This was about the time when Dr. Michael Cook (rabbi and renowned expert history of Passion plays around the world, and faculty member at the Hebrew Union seminary in Cincinnati) was asked, along with two other rabbis and four Catholic experts to review the script that had already been made into the movie as we now have seen it.[1]

Then there were the pre-screening clips shared with specially invited groups of Christian clergy. Those who saw these clips – and some who saw the whole movie in its thus-far-completed form – were enjoined to sign confidentiality oaths, except for those who were going to praise the film.

Then there were interviews with Gibson and reports about extreme religious events that occurred on the set and in and around the locales where the movie was shot.[2]

Then came the sad exposure of the bigotry of Hutton Gibson, Mel Gibson's father. Much later, Mel was interviewed by Diane Sawyer for ABC television, where he indirectly repudiated what his father believes but not his father.

Then there were the pre-screenings at major venues among conservative Christians and other groups such as at the Christian Broadcasters Convention, and then the overall marketing strategy Gibson used to influence evangelical churches toward building a momentum of anticipation and interest in the movie.

And then the Madness of March, Gibson's effort has paid off with a big, big response. In true American success story tradition, Gibson's *"The Passion..."* movie is a runaway hit. Since its release, it's taken in gross receipts of an average of $10,000,000 per day. The buzz has been extraordinary. For each sermon I prepare for you here at Community, I have a folder, after the example James Wallace Hamilton. And into each folder, like this one, I place articles, ideas, stories, magazine pieces, anecdotes. This is the folder today's sermon, representing the most printed material I have I've witnessed come my way regarding a religious event in our culture. As I said, the buzz has been extraordinary. And I will not be surprised if history eventually records that more than 10 billion words were written, reported, and preached in response to Gibson's cinematic interpretation of Jesus' last twelve hours of earthly life.

About the Movie

We may ask, we should ask now, to quote another famous movie and Broadway show about Jesus, *"What's the buzz, tell [us] what's happenin'!"*

Simply put, Gibson's movie is an emotionally wrenching portrayal of Mel Gibson's interpretation of some portions of the New Testament, traditionally called the "passion" narratives. Gibson has gone to pains to include the Seven Last Words of Christ from the Cross, all of which have their origins in the New Testament. Three of the Seven Last Words come from the gospel according to John, three come from the gospel according to Luke, and one is from the shared source of Matthew and Mark's gospels.

Gibson's vivid portrayal of the passion – the name of which, like the tradition, comes from the Latin word for suffering, *passio* – is also a depiction of several sources that do not have their origins in the New Testament, including the 14 stations of the Cross, along with the reveries of French mystic nun Anne Catherine Emmerich (1774-1824), whose visions of the original Calvary scenes were written down by Charles Brentano.

Note also these aspects on Mel Gibson himself.

About Mel Gibson

Mr. Gibson is a Catholic who has a quarrel with his church. He doesn't respect the changes brought about by Pope John XXIII through the Second Vatican Council. He prefers the manner of Catholic observance including the rendering of the Mass completely in Latin, and with the priest's back to the congregation. Gibson, according to his own self-revelations on Ms. Sawyer's show and others', has overcome a series of challenging addictions and less than noble stints in his life. In the process, recently he has undergone a religious awakening and spiritual transformation, as he tells it, with a new understanding and appreciation for the Christian faith.

Note with me now some items of interest about...us.

About Us

Somehow this movie has struck a deep chord within the American psyche. Perhaps it is because of a deep hunger for significance. Perhaps it has tapped into a deep thirst for meaning. Perhaps it is because we have been starving for something or religious significance and meaning to make its way into our pop cultural priorities, which is a natural yearning but not necessarily, in the end, a healthy one. Since what is pop can go pop and fizzle out all together. For example, *The Kansas City Star* ran a contest (a championship modeled after the 64-team field of the NCAA men's basketball brackets) asking for readers to choose "the most memorable moment in the past 50 years."[3] Only one religious figure or event made it into the top 64 pop cultural events/celebrities of the past 50 years: Jimmy Swaggart.

Surely it isn't coincidental that in a society that has been so induced to fear – by terrorism and our responses to that sad fact, nationally, regionally, municipally, and individually – we have responded with great emotion to a movie that has the capacity to heighten fear and deepen remorse. Our images of God and

Christ have been too much like H. Richard Niebuhr described some 60 years ago: *"A God without wrath brought men without sin into a kingdom without judgement through the ministrations of a Christ without a cross."*[4] Gibson's movie directly confronts that facile understanding of Christ's salvific work.

Again, what how Gibson's movie version of the Passion has affected us has to do with what movies do to us and how they do it.

Please note with me...

What Movies Do –

(1) ***Movies, perhaps more pointedly than other story-telling vehicles, entertain.*** That is, they cause us to smile, or to be intrigued, or to escape drudgery, or to stimulate our yearnings for happiness and good relations.

(2) ***Movies, like all art, excite our emotions.*** Movies tease us, titillate us, shock us, sadden us, inspire us, thrill us, bore us, electrify us. They give us silly scenes to laugh or scoff at and they offer us instances of nobility that move us to tears of admiration. Movies manipulate us, when we let them, toward new, different, strange, emotive states of being in the world.

(3) ***Movies allow us the hint of an omniscient, "God-like" perspective*** on and in the world, going where our eyes and ears and attention cannot normally nor easily go. Movies peer into the deep recesses of prisons, bore into the earth's core, transport us to different cultures. Movies compel us to go, as the matron in the play "Our Town" admonishes a young up-start to go, "to go to a place where they don't speak your language." How many Christians, for example, had ever witnessed Southern Pentecostalism before they went to see Robert Duvall's portrayal of E.F. ("Sonny") Dewey in the movie *The Apostle*?

(4) ***Movies – like newspapers, television and books also do – provide us with a common vocabulary and common reference***

points for historical understanding and popular culture awareness. Many of you will recall how the generations born after World War II, along with their children, have gained new perspectives on the genesis for traditional patriotism, as well as the unrelenting anguish that haunts many former soldiers, because of *Saving Private Ryan*. And a society that once avoided any exposure of or talk about prejudice toward Jews cannot as easily avoid that discussion now, not since Steven Spielberg's masterpiece, *Schindler's List*. Movies allow certain cultural experiences to be included in the world views of those who read less and less in the United States.

Note with me also...

How Movies Do What They Do

How movies do what they do is equally significant. Through a combination of image and sound, light and shadow, action and stillness, movies impress messages and meanings upon us.

Unlike reading matter, which allows our imaginations to run rampant with our own images of what a character named "Boo Radley" looks like (in *To Kill A Mockingbird*), ***movies give us the "template" or visual standard,*** if you will, for not only what "Boo Radley" looks like, but how he moves through the world, what his actual posture and demeanor are.

Unlike the still visual arts – which are attended either by the normal sounds that echo throughout a gallery hallway or by the normal sounds of one's household as one gazes an art book – ***movies provide the sounds for us.*** Surrounding us with darkness, they insulate us from the normal. They provide a sensory cocoon by which our regular world is kept away, if only for a couple of hours, from our normal awareness.

At the same time, they provide us an alternative world in which what happens on a screen somehow happens in and to

us. Movies, in this regard, can be equally powerful as a route for escapism or a road toward engagement.

Some Assessments

However you've reacted to the movie – either it's phenomenal presence in our culture or the very movie itself in the theater – allow me to affirm the experience you've had. My main response is: ***"If you thought the movie was powerful, you ought to read the book!"***

There is a wide variety of assessment by regular moviegoers like you and me and among the professionals who review movies from every possible angle. Richard Corliss is right, I think, to call it *"The Goriest Story Ever Told."*[5] As is David Denby, who, in the same light, has called it *"a gore fest."*[6] Andrew Sullivan has termed it *"pornography"* and offers this, "the kindest thing that may be said of Gibson is that he is an extremely late medieval."[7] And a rabbi colleague wrote in the local Jewish Chronicle that *"If Gibson is ever going to win any awards for his private project, it should be for advertisement and PR."*[8]

Conclusions

(5) ***It is after all a movie and an incomplete one at that.*** First it is incomplete in its accuracy. It misplays Caiphas, as a premier example, I believe. Caiphas was never the villainous bloodthirsty leader of the Sanhedrin as portrayed in this film. There are no Biblical or historical accounts that say Caiphas rode a donkey to the crucifixion or taunted Jesus on the cross. Some anti-Semitic Passion plays in Europe do that – the ones Hitler used to attend and exploit for his purpose as he built up the juggernaut of Nazi Germany. It is also incomplete as to its violence and the perpetrators of it in reference to Jesus. Pilate, to use the reviewer's vernacular, gets a pass, but the brutal, blood-fest of a scourging, which occupies less than a sentence in any gospel account, goes on interminably.

(6) ***It should never be a test of faith for any Christian.*** Some have attempted to make it so, and this is unfortunate. If any one ever seems to want to make "The Passion..." movie a test of faith–if you are really a Christian, then you'll see this as the 'greatest evangelism tool to come along in the last millennial!'" ... Hogwash! The greatest evangelism tool remains what it has always been, as D.T. Niles famously declared once: ***"It is one beggar telling another beggar where to get bread."***

Now the movie does have the power, I believe, to deepen the faith of a person who is already a Christian. But for those who uncommitted, especially those who are not connected to any faith whatsoever, they will not get the story in all of its fullness nor the meaning of the cross in all of its dimensions.

(7) ***It is a titanic failure***–mostly because it frames the passion–the deathly last 12 hours of Jesus' life on earth with very little context.

Oh, yes there are some flash back scenes–but only fleeting, too fleeting for my faith–but they fail to give the texture of Jesus' life and ministry. And there is a short shrifting of the resurrection. Yes, Jesus does get up from the tomb, with the "shroud of Turin," supposedly, fluttering in the background on the tomb bier.

What Gibson's movie misses the most is the important theme and absolutely necessary fact of "relationships" between Jesus and his followers. Relationships, this is what Jesus was always about.

This is what Paul emphasized again, and again: *"God...reconciled us to himself through Christ...and has given us the ministry of reconciliation"* (2 Cor. 5:18). And this is what all the post-resurrection scenes are all about: The resurrection is not only about Jesus' overcoming of death and ultimate vindication. The resurrection is always about the relationships we share with one another. As you have heard this morning, *"...we know that the one who raised the Lord Jesus will raise us also with Jesus."*

A Word of Thanks

In its failure of a titanic proportion, let us admit that, still, Mr. Gibson has done us a service, or at least we can see a service he has done, whether he intended to or not.

He has increased dialogue about the importance of faith and its place in our lives. This coming Palm Sunday, when we listen to the great music to be presented by the Chancel Choir and the Holiday orchestra, as well as on Wednesday, Thursday, and Good Friday services, I will join you in leaning into the many nuances of the Calvary and seek a deeper understanding of Christ's work in our hearts.

When someone was mad during medieval times, they were said to be "touched." Well, maybe that's right. However far flung Gibson's theology may be, may we always be touched by the hand of the divine. Love to you all as we touch the wall which is to be re-consecrated, as we touch each other with reassuring love and as we proceed to a much more sensitive understanding of the Passion in and out of the movie house, the Bible and within our souls. AMEN.

Notes

1 From a lecture by Dr. Cook, March 22, 2004, Interfaith Clergy Institute, St. Luke's Hospital, Kansas City, Missouri

2 In a widely circulated piece by Paul Harvey, it was said by David Limbaugh that Gibson reported *"Everyone who worked on this movie was changed. There were agnostics and Muslims on set converting to Christianity...[and] people healed of diseases."*

3 "Pop Culture," *The Kansas City Star*, *FYI* section, March 20, 2004, E1

4 Quoted in Kenneth L. Woodard, *"Do You Recognize this Jesus?"* February 25, 2004, *The New York Times.*

5 Richard Corliss, *"The Goriest Story Every Told," Time*, March 1, 2004, pp. 64-65.

6 David Denby, "Nailed," The New Yorker, March 1, 2004

7 Andrew Sullivan, *The New Republic*, February 26, 2004

8 Rabbi Jacques Cukierkorn, *"Dispassionate about 'The Passion'," The Kansas City Jewish Chronicle*, February 27, 2004, p. 23.

11

Shhh... (A Baccalaureate Sermon)

Text: Deuteronomy 6:4-5

Many thanks to President Sellars, Board Chairman John Beuerlein, and the Drury community for the gracious welcome and to Rev. David Bolling a special word of thanks for the warm hospitality. And to Karen Sweeny, deepest thanks, but I must admit I'm not exactly sure what to do with such an introduction. I think I'll take it home with me to show my wife whom she's married to.

Now, before I forget, "Happy Mothers Day!" And to be an equal opportunity greeting, in anticipation of next month's festivities, "Happy Fathers Day" too! With all due respect to the liturgical purists among us who would have us eschew any and all cultural references in worship – especially something as traditional – and sometimes more than a bit sentimental – as our Mothers Days have become and our Fathers Day celebrations occasionally are – this morning must include a nod of recognition to those who gave birth to and footed the bills and prayed for the achievements of those who "will walk" this afternoon in graduation ceremonies. Consider my Mothers and Fathers Day salutation as merely another moment of fulfilling the fifth of the ten commandments, *"Honor your father and your mother..."* (Ex. 20:12). And let us remember the Yiddish proverb, with a twist, *"Because God could not be everywhere, God made mothers and fathers."* So, "Happy Mothers Day!" and "Happy Father's Day!" too.

But secondly, and most appropriately, "Congratulations!" to all of you graduates. What a gracious moment this is. It's all over now. It's complete. *Finis*. Done. The bull is in the barn. The curtain has dropped. That last paper is in and you have now concluded this first phase of your life-long education. "Congratulations!" Yes, what a gracious moment this is.

But because you are only finished with *this* phase of your education and not finished for life, because you may be done with classroom work here at Drury, but *not yet done* with the living of your days, there is a word, a fresh word, I believe, for you and me and for all mothers and fathers and sisters and brothers, indeed for all our kin and for all people.

There is a text, well known by us all, that speaks directly to the achievements of a life lived well, to the commencement of new adventures, and to the central question of what really matters. The text to which I refer is at the heart of Christianity.

It is ***the main faith impulse*** for those who would follow Jesus.

It is ***the touchstone*** by which Christians know their richest heritage.

It is ***the foundation*** of everything that Jesus stood for, taught, and embodied.

It is ***the constituting moment*** for Judaism out of which Christianity was birthed.

It is ***the essence of Christian faith***, as it is lived out in the context of a caring church.

We call it *"The Great Commandment"*. Jesus said all the law and the prophets depended upon it and were bound together by it. Hear once again this precious text from Deuteronomy– *"Hear O Israel, the Lord our God, the Lord is One. And you shall love the Lord, your God with all your heart and with all your soul, and with all your might."*

How important is this text? Victor Frankl was the founder of the school of psychology called logotherapy, an understanding of humanity and humanity's search for meaning. Frankl forged this mode of thinking out of his World War II experiences as a prisoner in Nazi concentration camps, including Auschwitz, where he would survive, even though he would witness his father's death.

The story is told of Frankl's treatment when he first arrived at Auschwitz.[1] Like all Jewish prisoners were required to do, he had to shed himself of all his possessions, including his shoes, glasses and all his clothes. He had sewn into his clothes his most valuable treasure, a manuscript for a volume that he hoped to complete, *The Doctor and the Soul*. When the prison officials demanded that he disrobe, he begged to keep his coat which hid his valuable manuscript. They scoffed and repeated the demand with vehemence. He did as he was commanded, and shed himself of his clothes and thus his life's work and, as he says in his famous book *Man's Search for Meaning*, *"struck out my whole former life."*[2]

They would eventually give Frankl some other clothes, other prisoner's clothes, ragged and tattered. When he put his prison garb on, he found something hidden in a pocket. It was a portion of a Hebrew prayer book, a mere scrap of paper. And how did the ragged piece of prayer book read? *"Hear O Israel, the Lord our God, the Lord is one. And you shall love the Lord, your God with all your heart, with all your soul, and with all your might."* In place of his life's work, he had received that which would truly equip him for the work of life. *"Those words became for Frankl, a calling. And through horrible suffering they became for him a key for becoming whole, for staying centered. In all that you do, through all that you do, with all that you are: Hear, O Israel, the Lord our God, the Lord is one. And you shall love the Lord, your God with all your heart, with all your soul, and with all your [might]."*[3]

This morning, I'm here simply to remind each of you to love God with all your heart, soul and might, and, for just a few brief moments, to place a reminding emphasis on how this sacred text relates to this day of holy closure and new beginnings. Here the text once more: *"Hear O Israel, the Lord our God, the Lord is One. And you shall love the Lord, your God with all your heart and with all your soul, and with all your might."*

That says it all, doesn't it? Jesus thought so.

"And you shall love the Lord, your God..." with everything you have or know.

Love God – more than prestige, power, or position.

Love God – more than wealth or health or comfort or privileged condition.

Love God – more than country or country club or tribe or nostalgic time or hometown team or even origin.

Of course, we know that Jesus coupled the truth from Deuteronomy with its logical consequence; the best way to show one's love of divinity is by loving humanity. The best way to show we love God is by loving neighbor – neighbors who are friends – and neighbors who are strangers; neighbors we like and neighbors we not sure we'll ever like.

Now, we know that love moves us to coo with warm affection when parents bring their babies before the congregation for blessing and dedication.

Love inspires us to act with courage and in congruence with our best selves, causing even the crustiest souls to become loving and gentle.

Love is the motivation and destination behind all of our preparations and traditions.

Love is what warms our homes and our hearts even in the middle of life's iciest chills.

Love is tough resistance in the face of any thing or force which would bruise or hurt or harm.

Love is the peace that abides when we let go of old habits and encrusted conventions that hinder creative growth in our individual and collective lives.

Love abides when we vigorously challenge one another to live out our best ideals.

Love is undeniably front and center in the face of any child of God who is unafraid to tell the truth.

Love is generative, moving us to seek and to offer forgiveness when estrangement has occurred.

Love is protective, moving us to provide sheltering kindness for the least, the lost and the lonely among us.

Love is baking a pie, writing a note, praying a petition, organizing a worthy project, sitting in silent vigil at the bedside with patient, earnest hope: without love, such caring acts become mere drudgery.

Love is telling children of your joy in them, complimenting someone about a new haircut, expressing thanks for someone's unique talents: without love, such transactions are mere rote rituals or, worse, sham-filled facades.

Love, God's love, love as it has been given to the world

through the birth of a baby in Bethlehem long ago, love as it was made manifest on a cross and in an empty tomb, love as it is being given to new hearts even now–all of this love constitutes the reason for faith itself.

Love is truly at the heart of the way of Jesus.

But here allow me to note something that is paramount and patently clear to us all: love is hard. Sometimes it may even seem impossible. In a culture and a time in history with so many other loyalties pulling at us, loving God with all our heart, soul and might, and our neighbors as ourselves is one tall, tall order.

Graduates, if–or better said–***when*** those times come in your evolving life, cut yourself some slack. When the heart breaks, and the soul seems dim, and the might wanes, know that God was supremely wise in instructing Moses to say the great commandment in the way he did. Sometimes, say, like on a particularly brutal Thursday afternoon, it's sometimes just not possible nor practical nor even feasible that a "human merely being" (to use e.e. cummings' telling phrase) can love God in totality. That's all right. Notice that before the command to love God, there is the declaration of the unity of God: ***"...the Lord our God, the Lord is one...,"*** the monotheistic genius of the Judeo-Christian heritage.

No longer was there then nor is there now any need for the little demi-gods before which we worship. Paul Scherer once described the occasion of a worship service like this morning's gathering as *"that moment when we bring all the little gods we have made into the presence of the one God who made us."*

Little gods like...our appearance or our popularity or our place or even our own religion. Little gods like...security, national or personal, or salvation through entertainment or Wall Street or social climbing.

But the text says there is only one God, the Lord. And that can make for a lot less confusion, heartache, and daily trouble. In the place of our modern polytheism, the Shema calls us to rely upon the God who is God only and alone.

But, you say, in these uncertain times, that's another tall order. You're right! Some hard-pressed Wednesday afternoons, say, fidelity to God–to God alone and only–just might seem impossible.

Have no fear, however. Before the declaration about the oneness of God, there is the identification of the community of faith–*"O Israel."*

Sometimes when it seems like the height of hubristic folly–to love God, the king of the universe, the Unmoved Mover, the Creator of the Cosmos, the Lord of Life, the One, True God, the All in All–sometimes when it seems impossible to grasp the oneness of God, it may be the best we can do is to remember the sacredness of the community of faith. *"O Israel,"* the text says. O Israel, O God's people, the people whom God loved, the people of faith, those without whom our lives would lose their savor and the future would lose its purpose.

Allow me a substitute, a synonym for the phrase *"O Israel."* For the followers of Jesus, after a sufficient number of seasons in the Church, one of the most sacred words in the Christian vocabulary is ***"Congregation."*** *"Congregation,"* we say when our hearts are bursting with good news–when the engagement is announced, when the graduation–at long last–happens, when the baby is born.

Sarah Van Horn, one of the members of the diaconate at Community, once told me a telling story about the importance of "congregation." She said that before arriving at Community she hadn't much darkened the door of a church, except for a few weddings, including her own to Mike, her husband now of nearly 20 years. But then the baby came. And she found herself in the midst of a group of people in a building with a table in the middle of it, with a cross above it. In this group, people shared their faith together. It was a special place, a special group, a bit strange, to tell you the truth, the only place where people sang out loud together and prayed together and generally shared their greatest intimacies together.

And so I asked her, "Why did you come back to church after all those years? Was it that you wanted to be a good parent, that you needed help in that department?"

"No, not really," she said.

"Well," I pressed on, "was it nostalgia that drew you back?"

"No, not that at all."

"Well," giving up, I finally asked, "What was it?"

"I just had to thank some one," Sarah said, as she looked down at her son Nate. "I just had to thank somebody, and this seemed like a wonderful group of people with whom to share our joy."

"Congregation"–people of God–*"O Israel."* Such comforting words–in the midst of heartache–when the job goes bad, when the diagnosis says "cancer," when the depression descends, when the loved one is lost.

Where else do we go at such times, but into the gracious embrace of the congregation? *"Congregation"*–people of God–*"O Israel."* Yes, a holy word that is not merely the object of Moses' instructions on behalf of the Lord, but also a sacred reminder of the mediator of God's love in Christ, Christ's very Body, the Church.

Now, again, if we are bluntly honest, even *"congregation"*–good old "Israel"–is a bit much to take on occasion. (Here, I am reminded of what my good friend Rabbi Michael Zedek once taught me about the twin temptations faced by every religious leader. There's the temptation of Aaron to love the people a whole lot more than you love God. And then there's the temptation of Moses to love God a whole lot more than you love the people. The trick is to keep the two in balance.)

There will come times, say, on a hard and bitter Monday afternoon, when a connection with the congregation will not do. Sometimes all of us–even the ones who love the Church more than they have words to express–experience difficulties mustering energy to say the word "congregation" with absolute appreciation. That's OK, by the way. In fact, it's A-OK. Once more, Moses, inspired by God's powerful, holy presence, provides a safety net in the very text of Deuteronomy 6:4-5. Before the mandate to love God, before the declaration of God's oneness, and prior to pronouncing the sacred name of the congregation, there is a simple, direct, codified commandment that God wants God's people to follow. So on a Monday, before loving God, prior to declaring the oneness of God, before pronouncing the sacred name "congregation," you are to... ***"Hear!"***

This is a primary task. This is an absolute spiritual necessity for followers of Jesus Christ. This is the fundament of faith. *"Hear!"*

And may you remember to hear God in your lives by remembering this text from Deuteronomy and the name given to it by tradition. In Hebrew it's called simply, and sacredly, the ***"Shema,"*** after the first word of the fourth verse of the sixth chapter of Deuteronomy. *"Shema, O Israel..." "Hear, O Israel..."*

Hear, listen, pay attention. I call it an ***"onomatopoeic aspirant"*** because you can hear in Hebrew the meaning which is easily discernable, amazingly enough, in English: *"Shema..." "She..." "Sh..." "Shhhhh!" "Hear!" "Listen!"*

Why "Hear"? I'm glad you asked that question. Because that's how God first expressed divine power at the dawn of all beginnings. When God leaned over the balcony of all possibility, God did what? God spoke!

No creation with lightning bolts of electric splendor or with mega watts of physical power. No brilliant display of technicolor glory. No visual cipher in a written text.

How did God first create at Eden's dawning? With basic words that were uttered with great grace and the expectation that they would be heard: *"Let there be!"* Thus, we are to hear!

And thus we are to be quiet with our puny complaints, with our incessant self-absorption. Instead, hear, listen to God's voice. Hear, listen to God speaking in and to your own lives.

Hear...the whisper of the dispossessed crying in the night.

Hear...the shouts of the glad ones tasting freedom for the first time.

Hear...the despairing masses who are numbered among the world's poor.

Hear...the chatter of modern Americans who really yearn to speak in more meaningful ways.

Hear...the questions of children.

Hear...the desire for support for the elderly.

Hear...the beating hearts of all of God's people.

Hear...the laughter at your own wonderment and your own foolishness, sometimes in the same instance.

Hear...the welling gratitude bubbling up wherever and whenever God's people are engaged in worthy struggle.

Hear...the joy that comes when truth is made plain and justice reigns and love knows limit in the human community.

So...Remember...***Love God!***

Recall—as often as you can—***The Lord is One!***

Say the saving word ***"Congregation"*** with renewed appreciation.

And ***"Hear!"***—let the voice of God speak to your hearts.

And if you will do this, you will come to a new time in your life as a graduate of Drury University, and as a child of God, when you'll know that the best days are ahead of you. May you begin in that knowledge even now, right now, today. And, of course, tomorrow, on Monday, you may want to remember.... *Shema! Hear! Shhhhhh....!* AMEN

Notes

1 I'm thankful to Rev. Barbara Blaisdell for a reminder about this event in Frankl's life. This scene is also described by Rabbi David Aaron in his piece entitled "*How living the commandments empowers you to connect with God and be your true self*" at www.aish.com/spirituality/philosophy/Channeling_Spiritual_Light.asp

2 *Man's Search for Meaning: An Introduction to Logotherapy*, (New York: Washington Square Press, 1965), p. 21.

3 Rev. Barbara S. Blaisdell, Hilo Coast U.C.C., Honomu, HI, April 2, 2006, *The Gospel Unhindered: A Bible Study on the Book of Acts, Lent 2006, "Unhindering Divided Hearts."*

12

Of Callings, Canyons & Christian Enduring

Texts: 1 Samuel 3:1; Psalm 84; Acts 16:11-15

On the Occasion of the Ordination of The Rev. Sunny Buchanan

Sunny Buchanan, we are blessed by your response to God's call on your life! Christian Church (Disciples of Christ), what a blessing it is to gather together for this day of celebration, this occasion of gifting the world and the Church with a stellar leader which it so direly needs at such a time as this. And Church of Jesus Christ, ready or not, Sunny Buchanan is about to bless you!

The ordination of any minister, and this one soon to be called "Rev. Sunny Buchanan," inspires us to ponder the "calling" of a minister. And, as we ponder that mysterious experience called "calling," we may happen upon some insights about "canyons" and maybe even about "Christian enduring."

Of Callings

A "calling" is, of course, what a vocation is all about. Vocation itself means, in its Latinate origins, "to call." Frederick

Buechner has pretty much provided the best definition ever of what vocation and calling are all about when he says: "The place God calls you to is the place where your deep gladness and the worlds deep hunger meet."

Sunny Buchanan has discerned that her deep gladness will be found, has already been found in a life of leadership and the sharing of her gifts and graces in a congregation of the Church of Jesus Christ. And there is a concomitant hunger–a deep, nearly ravenous hunger sometimes–on the part of the Church and the world for such leadership and such gifts and graces. Truly Sunny, your calling, we perceive and have told you, is a true and appropriate thing. It, the calling, and you, the called, are so right. And thus this service today is a good and gracious thing to enact.

But Buechner's definition doesn't exhaust the many meanings that your calling has had for you, nor the meanings that any calling has for any ordained minister. Nor does Buechner's definition bespeak of the extraordinary depths of mystery that attend this thing called "calling."

The text from Samuel gets a little closer. Samuel, a young person, hears a voice in the night and thinks it is old Eli calling him to some sort of service. Old Eli, after a while, figures out it is the Lord God Almighty, and gives Samuel a formulaic response the next time Samuel happens to detect a similar call upon his attention. And so, Samuel does as Eli instructs him. "And the LORD came and stood forth, calling as at other times, 'Samuel! Samuel!' And Samuel said, 'Speak, for thy servant hears.'"

Samuel's call is not unlike the perduring, persistent, pesky call that so many have sensed in their lives. They hear but they cannot quite listen to the exact claim on their lives. They run to a mentor, or to a career, or to a guru, or to a sideline bet on a different path. Or they become willfully deaf and refuse to hear that voice call out "Samuel, Samuel,...Sunny, Sunny."

But the day comes when it all comes clear and there is a response, OK I'll be your minister, I'll wear that mantle, put the stole upon me, send me forth. And another ordained minister is commissioned and sent forth.

Sunny, today it is my responsibility – on behalf of this congregation, on behalf of the congregations where you have grown up and heard the call, and the congregations where you will serve from this day forward – to remind you, to remind myself, to remind all of us, of Old Eli's wise, charming, saving direction which Samuel enacted in responding to his call. "And Samuel said, 'Speak, for thy servant hears.'" Not "Listen up God, not listen up God, listen up Church, I've got something to say." But rather, in the tradition ol' Eli, 'Speak, for thy servant hears.'"

Which means that the constant task of an ordained minister – from the very beginning onward – is to listen, listen, listen, carefully, particularly to God.

The ordained ministerial life is listening life. Listening to the call and claim of God on your existence. Listening to the cries of the world's deep hungers. Listening to your own deep gladness.

And in such a listening, surely you will hear how you are to do not merely passable work, not merely an acceptable fulfillment of your tasks as a minister. No, Sunny, if we know you half as much as we think we know you, and if we reckon honestly with the abundance of loving gifts with which God has graced you, we would surely declare that you are called Sunny Buchanan to do great work, great teaching, great preaching, great healing, great wholeness work on behalf of the gospel of God in Jesus Christ.

This kind of sacral listening means not only listening so as to hear your own calling and be reminded of it throughout your life. It also mans to help others–the members of the churches wherever you serve–to listen to the callings in their lives. Your calling means that you are charged with the holy duty of leading others to tune in to their own callings.

Yes calling. Being ordained is all about the mysteries of our "callings." But it is more.

Of Canyons

The life of an ordained minister may be likened unto a trip to Grand Canyon. At some point, at a certain time, in the clutch of a crisis or the strain of a stress, or at the alpine heights of jubilation and joy, someone, normally a church member, or one becoming so, will draw you aside, and say, "Come over here, I've got something to show you." Then they'll put their arm around your shoulder and point and say, "See, isn't it wonderful?!"

And there before you is an awe-inspiring scene. It's the "Grand Canyon" of their life–with all of its stratified record of past deluge moments when they were drowning in some existential horror, and yet emerged safe and saved and whole. And there's a series of deep crevices, cut by years of weary wearing away. Down, down the canyon walls, way down at the bottom at the *sipapu,* from which, as the Anasazi tribes believe, the First People entered the current world from the Lower World, you can see your church member's origins, what gave them life and a destiny and the stuff that makes them "them" and not someone else.

There are beautiful turns at head waters where the Grand Canyon of their lives begin, and there are absolutely breathtaking moments toward the western most edges of it, especially at the sunset times of their existence. And all of it is simply a gift, sheer grace. And your job, your ordained task as minister, is simply to share such a moment with them.

Then there are some other times, when they are shouting out to you, yearning for "Help, help, help!" Sometimes they might even be screaming in abject helplessness. And you go over to the rim of the Grand Canyon of their lives, and they are holding on for dear life by their fingernails to the painful edge of that rim. And you reach down and pull them out. Sometimes their predicament is such it may be necessary for you to have some assistance in pulling them out of harm's way or their own self-pity or their reckoning with their dashed dreams or their failed hopes or their own personal dissolution, however it comes. This too is ministry of the most basic and most blessed kind.

I used to think that's what ministry consisted of–the rare and graced occasion of sharing in the "Grand Canyon" dimensions of people's lives. And I still do believe that's a big part of it. But I've also come to know that such a one-directional view in this "Grand Canyon" metaphor won't do. It's not thorough enough. It's not whole. There's a another directional view to add. It's like this. There's the "Grand Canyon" experiences that church folks share with an ordained minister, and there's the "Grand Canyon" moments of seeming helplessness when our members want and need so desperately to be pulled off the precipice. And, then there are those moments when we ordained ones take our church members by the hand and put our arm around their shoulder and show them the "Grand Canyons" of our lives. And sometimes, usually at a critical time in the development use of our gifts, we cry out to our church members to come over to the rim of our "Grand Canyon," because we need so desperately need help to keep from falling down and in to whatever ill fate awaits us. And they share our awe in the face of the beautiful life that has been granted to us and they pull us out in the nick of time. Now that is truly what ministry has come to mean to me. In short, it's always a two-way street of gracing and gratitude, of healing and helping.

This is what the Psalmist is up to in Psalm 84: "How lovely is your dwelling place, O Lord of hosts!" What else can you say when confronted by the "Grand Canyon" dwelling places of our lives, both those of the faithful who make up the church's membership, and those who are its ordained leaders? How lovely indeed! And what can any of us ever do, when we've been retrieved from the canyon's edge and helped to stand once more and not fall, what else can we say but, "O Lord of hosts, happy is everyone who trusts in you"!!??

So Sunny, you may have thought that Grand Canyon was in Arizona, but I can tell you today, I know it's really in...-Livingston, Tennessee, and it's really in Nashville, Tennessee, and it's really in Blue Springs, Missouri, and it's really right here in Kansas City, and it's really in a myriad, countless other places, wherever the Church of Jesus Christ is. It will be wherever you go as an ordained minister. Wherever and whenever those "Grand Canyon" moments arise, get ready to say "How lovely is your dwelling place, O Lord of hosts!...O Lord of hosts, happy is everyone who trusts in you."

A Christian Enduring

The callings and the canyons of an ordained minister's life abide in an overarching context, of course. And there are few better revealings of that context than the story of Lydia's conversion and subsequent opening of her living room for the establishment of the first church in Europe.

In Dr. Luke's telling of Lydia's story, he paints the picture of one who listens, one who is then is personally persuaded and surrenders her will to God's will. She empowers her family, enlisting and enrolling them in the Christian story. She then"-prevails" on Paul & his entourage to stay in her home.

This is a turning point in the history of the Church. Up through the 15th chapter of the book of Acts, Luke tells the story of the church in the third person, frequently singular—"they did this, they did that." Or better, "he did one thing, she did another." In the 15th chapter, Luke starts using "we" language—first person, usually plural. And Lydia is part of this transition, what might also be called a transformation.

As Luke and the Church make the transforming transition from third person singular to first personal usually plural, Lydia is all a part of it. And she is so because she "prevails" on Paul and his entourage to stay with her and her family.

A question pops up: How did she prevail on them?

Various translations tangle with the meaning of this word *παρεβιασσατο*:

"She urged us to stay..."

"She constrained us..."

"She told us to go [to her house]"

But I like Eugene Peterson's version of this phrase in his Message rendition: "She wouldn't take no for an answer..." This really gets at the word's meaning for our time, what it means to profess our faith, to offer a persuasive argument for the gift of love and grace and life itself in the spirit of Jesus.

Sunny, you are no stranger to the truth that the world is full of "No's" and that which drags down and hurts and harms. You have studied it, fully and broadly at Vanderbilt. You have discussed it with our colleagues until the wee hours of the morning. You have teased out what it means to confront the "no's" of the world in and through the vehicle of care and comfort and compassion known as the congregation. You've heard it and dealt with it within the encouraging families of faith at

First Christian in Blue Springs, at Community, and at Woodmont in Nashville.

You know what a "No" looks like, feels like, and you know its potential force for ill and against good. But you also have within you – by birth and baptism and blessing – legacy of Lydia, who will be your guide and inspiration in the days ahead as you engage in a holy "enduring." You have Lydia, as one your balcony people, as Carlyle Marney used to describe it, urging you, cheering your efforts of "Not taking 'No' for an answer."

Your "enduring" in the world and sometimes even in the Church – coupled with that of a whole new generation of clergy coming up through the ranks, (witnessed this day by your fine colleagues who parachuted into Kansas City for this occasion!) – may even be the beginning of a new turning point in the history of the Church, beginning with the Christian Church (Disciples of Christ) and then to who knows what other points beyond. Who knows.

What I do know is this: the world, and the Church especially, need your persuasive, compelling, enduring ways so it, so we, can "Yes" to an invitation to the lively Christian gospel. So, Sunny, remember Lydia's enduring ways, and how she wouldn't take "No" for answer.

A Final Word

One final word. The callings and the canyons and the context of Christian enduring are to be infused by your remembrance, Sunny, of a distinct piece of architecture at Vanderbilt Divinity School. On the inside of quadrangle around from the corner where you enter Benton Chapel and right outside the window of the refectory, there is a portion of the old divinity school. It's a triangular-shaped piece of old stone upon which is chiseled *"SCHOOL OF THE PROPHETS."*[1] You have now graduated—with distinction and in the shining light of our admiring pride!—from Vanderbilt Divinity School. We are thrilled. And we all know you are relieved! Yes, you have graduated from one of the best schools anywhere for ministerial preparation. You have the diploma to prove it. And so, understandably, you have left Vanderbilt.

But even so, may I beseech you, may I implore you, may I prevail upon you, never ever to leave the "School of the Prophets." The world needs you to be a constant student in the School of the Prophets. The Church is crying for one who is still in the School of the Prophets and can lead it to a new vibrancy and aliveness like it hasn't known in a long time. And you need it too, to be consistently and constantly schooled in the ever-revealing, ever-eye-opening, ever-soul-deepening insights of the prophets. So yes, you have left Vanderbilt. But we beseech you, the Church would prevail upon you: "Do not leave the School of the Prophets."

Sunny, as you remain true to your callings, and share in the extraordinary gifts of yet untold Grand Canyons, and abide in the spirit of Lydia, and do your proper studies in the school of the prophets, the Church will experience a transformation wherever you go, and the world, astonished by the good news which you will teach and preach and embody, will become a haven of hope, a sanctuary of salvation and a repository of righteousness. And don't we need it so! And don't we need you so! And, wow! Here you are! AMEN.

Notes

1 Dr. Jack Frostman, then Dean of The Divinity School of Vanderbilt University, first brought this to my attention and to the attention of the entire graduation class of 1980 in his commencement address.

13

When Second Best Is Better

Text: Acts 16:6-10

Our focus for this morning is on a seemingly small piece of scripture in the 16th chapter of the book of Acts. In this humble tale there are bold truths for us all. In the span of a mere five sentences and 104 words—in the English translation—a revolution occurs. Yes, a world-changing transformation happens. And it's all because of a failure. A second-rate occurrence, in a second-hand moment, for a second-tier religionist, in a second best town.

Now, admittedly, that's not what you heard when the story was read. You heard instead strange, super-Biblical-sounding words like "*Phrygia*" and "*Galatia*" and "*Mysia*" and "*Bithynia*" and "*Troas*"—words that nearly strike fear in the heart of even the best of all scripture readers, even preachers. But please, for a moment, use your sanctified imaginations at this point in our considerations and dip your fancy into the milieu of the early church and discover something new this morning.

Paul is commencing his second missionary journey. He

wants to go to Bithynia, to share the gospel. He has traversed the territory with Barnabas, and he's gathered Timothy in his wake and will very soon enroll Luke in his entourage. He has secured the proper letters of introduction from the apostles and elders in Jerusalem. He's set to go. And he yearns to make his way into Bithynia. And who wouldn't!?

Bithynia: a province of the Roman Empire that happened to be in Asia Minor, along the Black Sea, west of Pontus. It would become the site of early Christian groups. And it was a place of familiarity, a place of prominence, not only then, when Paul is commencing the trajectory of his second missionary journey, but later as well. It will be in the province of Bithynia that the historic council of Nicaea will be held in the year 325. And it will also be in Bithynia, in the year 451 that the great ecumenical Council of Chalcedon will be called to order.[1] Bithynia was, and would remain, in a word, "boss"!Or to use more contemporary parlance, Bithynia was "bad," so "bad" it was "the baddest." In a word Bithynia was the best.

Contrast Bithynia, then, with the lesser town of Troas. Troas–a coastal city and port on the Aegean Sea, a place typical of any Roman city at that time–theater, temple, baths, aqueducts. A town, not chosen at all by Paul to visit, let alone to evangelize and saturate with the good news of Jesus's gospel. A second choice, if that.[2]

Do you catch the difference?

Bithynia the bigger.

Troas the lesser.

Bithynia the familiar, with greater prestige.

Troas, the more unknown, the least.

Bithynia, the center of activity, the place of power and prominence, within the circles of the early church, for centuries really.

Troas, a mere passing-through promontory at best, a way-station, a toll-gate, not a "point of destination" at all.

Bithynia – first choice, best.

Troas – second-best, if that.

And what happens with Paul? He wants Bithynia, but he gets Troas.[3] And with that failure, with the power of the Holy Spirit moving him to Troas, and then, through the vehicle of a dream, beckoning him to come over to Macedonia, Paul manages to dramatically alter world history for all time.

We can never know what would have happened if Paul had been able to go to Bithynia; it's impossible to tell. But we know for certain what happened when Paul went through Troas to Macedonia. The gospel was spread to Europe for the first time, into Greece, into Italy, and eventually up to France, and over into Germany, and even up into the hinterlands of Gaelic and Celtic cultures and then to the world. Paul wanted Bithynia, but he got Troas, and the world was transformed for the better by the gospel ever thereafter!

We all know this experience of wanting Bithynia and getting Troas, it is an incontrovertible fact of our faith.

Robert H. Meneilly, who graced Community's pulpit just two weeks ago, is our dear friend, treasured mentor and exemplar to me in the ways of ministry. Robert Meneilly and his wife Shirley know what Bithynia and Troas are all about. Initially they wanted to go to China as Presbyterian missionaries. But it was not to be. Fresh out of Pittsburgh seminary, Bob and Shirley were sent elsewhere. Instead of the exotic environs of Shanghai or Canton or Beijing, they were privileged to receive the call to holy hamlet of...Prairie Village, Kansas. They may have wanted Canton, but they got Kansas.

A young Southerner named Bill also knew about the difference between Bythinia and Troas. Bill wanted to be a poet, and night and day he would slave away on his verse on the backside of a wheelbarrow in the basement boiler room of the university where he worked as a laborer. Romancing his time away, stanza after stanza. That was his "Bithynia"–to be the next American version of Shelley, Keats, Milton, or best of all, like the bard himself, Shakespeare. But he would fail at such a dream. And not very many of his poems got published. Instead he had to settle for Troas and thus he tried his hand at stories.

And a young man from Louisiana named Taylor yearned to be an attorney. To render spell-binding, spine-tingling orations in the sartorial splendor of the courtrooms of the American jurisprudence system. That was his "Bithynia." But a car accident–involving the death of two white men in the dark wiles of pre-World War II Louisiana–turned him toward his "Troas."

A young man named George was bound and determined to be and/or become a great baseball pitcher, the next Christy Matthewson. There were scouts that thought he just might do that. And there were batters who definitely thought he could do that. That was his "Bithynia;" it wasn't to be. Instead he would get "Troas."

To repeat, Paul wanted Bithynia, but he got Troas. He wanted the tried & true, the best & the brightest, the warm & the welcoming, the famous and the familiar Bithynia. Instead he got Troas. But, behold what he got when he *got* Troas!

- Because he went to Troas, he got the portal to the ultimate power chambers of Europe.
- Because he went to Troas, the gospel was transported out of the comfortable confines of the Mediterranean locales of Asia Minor.
- Because he went to Troas, the gospel of Jesus Christ got transmuted, translated, and transfigured into all the world.

Because Paul got the second-best destination for his assignment, the gospel got the best end of the deal. And so it has been with everyone who ever wanted the best of the "Bithynias" in their world, but instead got "Troas."

Robert and Shirley Meneilly may have wanted to be missionaries to China but instead they became the overseers of a burgeoning church in the humble hamlet of Prairie Village, Kansas, that would grow and grow and grow until they had 8,000 members, with a budget of $3,000,000, of which nearly half went to mission outreach work throughout the greater Kansas City area and around the world.

And young Bill the Southerner, the poet-wannabe, began trying his hand at stories. He got some published and then more. Then a novel and then a whole slew of novels about the slimy, servitude-bound Snopes family, and the achingly tragic Compson family–all of them in the renowned fictional Yauknapatapha County that would be known to the world when Bill, or William Faulkner, as the dust jackets of his books preferred to title him, would receive the Nobel prize for literature.

And the young African-American down in Louisiana, the one with lawyering on his mind, was acquitted of any crime. He had a deep conversation with himself and with God and then chose to pattern his life after his father and "make a preacher," a Baptist preacher at that, a renowned preacher at that, until at the ripe age of 34, he, Gardner C. Taylor, would assume the pulpit at the famed Concord Baptist Church of Christ in Brooklyn and hold forth for 42 years, becoming not only "the dean of the black pulpit" but the pre-eminent homiletical voice of the 20th century. And because he went to his "Troas" instead of "Bithynia," he would eventually preach the blessing sermons at the worship services marking two presidential inaugurations.

And that boy named George? Well, you know as well as I do that he was more a "babe" than a boy, and he would be changed from a pitcher into a hitter, his prowess with a bat being so overwhelmingly evident. And George Herman Ruth, the Babe, the Sultan of Swat, the Great Bambino, would not only serve himself well. In effect, after the scandals that rocked the baseball world following the World Series of 1919, he would save the essence of the game of baseball itself.

A Word of Encouragement about the Bithynias We Miss out On:

We need not complain too much or overlong about the doors to our Bithynias being closed to us. *Our Bithynias were never as perfect as our idealized fantasies about them anyway.*

Here are some words of wisdom for those who feel they've gotten a rotten deal in life:

- The best way to get even is to forget.
- Feed your faith & your doubts will starve to death.
- Some marriages are made in heaven, but all of them have to be maintained on earth.
- A successful marriage isn't finding the right person–it's being the right person.
- Sorrow looks back, worry looks around and faith looks up.
- Standing in the middle of the road is dangerous. You will get knocked down by the traffic from both ways.
- It isn't difficult to make a mountain out of a molehill–just add a little dirt.
- A skeptic is a person who, when he sees the handwriting on the wall, claims it's a forgery.
- The mighty oak tree was once a little nut that held its ground.
- To forgive is to set the prisoner free, and then discover the prisoner was you.
- You'll notice that a turtle only makes progress when it sticks out its neck.
- If the grass is greener on the other side of the fence, you can bet the water bill is higher.[4]

A Word of Reassurance and Challenge About Your Troas

When you miss out on your "Bithynia" but you're granted the invitation to a "Troas," see it for what it is: *a sometimes terrifying challenge that, if you will have the courage to engage in it, will be a place of ultimate fulfillment.* In this regard, I've always treasured the challenging dictate of W.E. Orchard who admonished us all with this motto:

And when the day goes hard,
and cowards steal from the field,
grant that our place may be found,
there where the fighting is fiercest.[5]

You might be a young woman with dreams and schemes of becoming the next Sandra Day O'Connor, but your choice of career endeavors doesn't match your opportunities. And besides you're allergic to legal pads. That's your "Bithynia." But a Vacation Bible School program with kids–kids who really need you and crave your creativity–turns into the most fulfilling challenge of your life. That's your "Troas."

Or you're a young man who dreams of becoming the next Warren Buffet of finance. But, despite the fact that your parents have always dreamed like you have, of a Harvard MBA, you normally have trouble balancing your checkbook. That's your "Bithynia." On the other hand, your knack for music and your love of children is calling to you, calling to a life of music education with third graders. That's your "Troas."

Or you're a man of high-powered intellect and you've always envisioned for yourself the upward trek of an ever-rising career. Bithynia. But you fall in love. And the woman of your dreams wants to make a family and has a career of her own. And somehow, without any nudging from her, but a little from the Holy Spirit, you get it in you're head you'll follow her career to Troas. And what about the family? You decide, instead of the career at Bithynia, you'll heed the call of being a house husband at Troas.

Or you're name is Betsy Colquitt, a top student in the English Department at Vanderbilt University. A darling of the department and the loquacious literati in Nashville, Tennessee. A rising star. Bithynia. But instead, you harken to the call to go to a place called TCU down in Ft. Worth, Texas. Troas. And at that Troas, you will become one of the most beloved, respected and influential teachers the school has ever known. At the "Troas" of TCU in Ft. Worth, Texas, you create poetry and inspire poets who will touch a nation.

Again, let me repeat: (1) *Our "Bithynias" were never as perfect as our idealized fantasies about them anyway. (2) And see your "Troas" for what it is: a sometimes terrifying challenge that, if you will have the courage to engage in it, can truly be a place of ultimate fulfillment.* Robert Frost's poetic genius put the entire matter this way: *"Two roads diverged in a yellow wood.../...and I,/ I took the one less traveled by,/ and that has made all the difference."*[6] Blessings on us all as we heed the call to Troas. Our willingness to allow God's Spirit to guide and shape our destinies makes all the difference in the world. AMEN.

Notes

1 See *Harpers Bible Dictionary*, by Madeleine S. Miller and J. Lane Miller (New York: Harper and Bros., 1952), p. 74; *Harpers Bible Dictionary*, Paul J. Achtemeier, gen.ed. (San Francisco: HarpersSanFrancisco, 1985), p. 135.

2 See *Harpers Bible Dictionary* (1952 edition), p. 786, & (1985 edition), p. 1009.

3 The phrase *"wanting Bithynia and getting Troas"* (the original inspiration for this sermon) is by Harry Emerson Fosdick in *The Hope of The World* (New York: Harper and Bros., 1933)

4 I recall Orchard's fetching phrase from an address by William Sloane Coffin in October, 1973, at the General Assembly of the Christian Church (Disciples of Christ) in Cincinnati. It can be found in *The Temple: A Book of Prayers* (London: J. M. Dent and Sons Ltd., 1913)

5 This list – in a another form, before adaptation – was forwarded by a friend via e-mail. If I ever had the name of the originator, I've since lost it.

6 From *"The Road Not Taken"* in *The Poetry of Robert Frost*, Edward Connery Lathem, ed. (New York: Henry Holt and Company, 1979), p. 105.

14

Training Up the Wise Child

Text: Proverbs 22:1-6

I. Introduction – Proverbs Aplenty

We're continuing our look at the powerful wisdom of the book of Proverbs, especially as it relates to training our children in the ways that they should live. From one perspective, the whole book of Proverbs can be understood as a training manual for the attainment of wisdom. Down through the Judeo-Christian heritage there has been a constant concern for the proper "raising up" of children. Good training makes for good families, good congregations, good neighborhoods, and a good society. There is an obvious, overarching concern for children within the book of Proverbs. Among the references to "a child" in the entirety of the Bible, 25% of them are in the book of Proverbs.

Of course, there's a tip-off at the very beginning, when the author states: "*Hear, my child, your father's instruction, and do not reject your mother's teaching...*" (1:8).

And again we hear: "*Hear, my child, and accept my words,*

that the years of your life may be many" (4:10).

And we even hear about the diet which children, and the rest of us, for that matter, should hold to: *"My child, eat honey, for it is good, and the drippings of the honeycomb are sweet to your taste"* (24:13).

And we learn too about the consequences for not following the wisdom of those instructing us when we are children: *"A child who loves wisdom makes a parent glad, but to keep company with [the false exploiters] is to squander one's substance"* (29:3).

Yes, there is an obvious, overarching concern for children within the book of Proverbs.

There are wisdoms we all live by, proverbs nearly, that we'd all want to pass along to the children among us. I'm grateful for so many of you passing along to me your best proverbial sayings and wise adages, by which you live your lives. And with permission granted to share these.

Dian McClymond reported that there's one saying that always stuck in her mind: *In discipline there is freedom*. It's not only memorable, it works! For, as Dian said so beautifully, *"It is so very simple–disciplined–but gives so very much to think about–freedom. It does not fail, whether organizing the junk drawer in the kitchen or dealing with far more important matters. Freedom is what we all want,...and discipline is a tool that is always within reach." In discipline there is freedom.* Yes, that's good.

Then there's a *"Roadtrip Mantra"* which has served Rene Morales well on thousands upon thousands of miles of driving trips. *"...in response to your request,"* Rene wrote via e-mail, *"for favorite proverb, wisdom, aphorism, watchword, or motto, here's mine: No animals, no accidents, no tickets."*

Rene utters that phrase to herself whenever she starts off on a roadtrip. And it's been very useful and effective for Rene.

"...this motto hasn't let me down yet."

Now I can't quote all of you, but I must cite one more, Jimmy Mohler, who, in her loquacious way, said tons, when she wrote, *"[Well here] are a few quotes and sayings that I have floating around my office to inspire."* One is anonymous and another is by Charles Henry Parkhurst.

"Not every flight needs a sky"–Anonymous.

"Sympathy is two hearts tugging at one load"–Charles Henry Parkhurst.

Others from Jimmy's collection is from before the time of Christ.

"Those who know how to win are much more numerous than those who know how to make proper use of their victories"–Polybius, historian (c. 205-123 BCE).

"To do nothing is sometimes a good remedy"–Hippocrates, physician (460-c.377 BCE).

And yet others of Jimmy's favorites are just singularly powerful.

"No snowflake ever falls in the wrong place"–Zen saying.

"If you don't find God in the next person you meet, it is a waste of time looking for him further"–Mahatma Gandhi (1869-1948).

"A friend is a single soul dwelling in two bodies"–Aristotle.

Not bad, not bad at all. Many if not most of those rank right up with the wisdom which the book of the Proverbs poses for children. We are all of us–from the ancient Hebrews to contemporary Christians–trying our bets to impart the best we know, whether comically rendered or rigidly somber, so the world, especially our children's parts in it, can be better.

Which leads me to suggest to us this morning that the book of Proverbs, and its emphasis on children and raising them up rightly, has caused me to ponder what words of wisdom might we want to emphasize in the raising up of the children whose care has been set to our hands.

When I think of words of wisdom, I'm hesitant to go beyond a few mere words. Instead of adages and aphorisms, I'll proffer here this morning some simple words, all but two of them single-syllable words, which every child should know. I entitle these...

"The Twelve Words Every Child Should Know By the Time They Are Twelve Years Old."

1–YES–This is a word that provides permission, affirmation and eventually celebration, in the midst of a world that is hell-bent-for-leather in denial, denigrating putdowns, and deadly boredom. Yes, that word that comes to the child's mind, and should, whenever loving arms embrace her, or a shining sun arises yet again one more morning, or the bottle approaches its landing in her mouth. Yes. Yes, this is the word we yearn to hear from children and adults when asked if they believe in Christ. Yes, the word we want them to say when the world knocks on their doors, years from now or tomorrow, with its seemingly incessant demands for justice and caring and maybe just simple food for the hungry. Yes, the life-giving, sensitive reflex when God asks who can He send to respond to the ravaging that goes on all too often.

2–NO–This is the word that parents teach to kids when young ones draw too close to the fire, or play too close to the street, or impulsively want too much before it's time for dinner. No is the little word with dynamite power. No, the word that negates, nullifies, and nixes, in the twinkling of an eye, especially when danger approaches. No, the word that a tyke learns has power, when he pleases himself to no end by refusing to participate in reasonable human activity. No, no, no, sometimes even spoken with a smile, not simply because it's such a splendidly easy word to pronounce, but because of its baffling power to render once capable adults into puddles of frustration. But this "No" is important too because it is one of religion's basic power words. No, we say, we don't do that here. No to discrimination. No to hate, not even within ourselves in response to the most despicable things others can hurl at us. No to drugs and No to promiscuity and No to the reckless stupidity of bullying others. No, that word, when used properly, is nearly an affirmation itself.

3–LOVE–Of course, you thought that this word would be first, but it can't not linguistically speaking. Yes, and no are commands and as such are absolutely appropriate for infancy. But then around one years old or one year and three months old, the cooing sounds of "I love you" begin to register, as they should, and this is the third word which children should know for sure. And they should learn it and repeat it and hear it repeated to them again and again and harbor it within their hearts. For it is in mastering this word, a truly life-long task that can never begin too soon, that leads to the proverbial "life worth living."

Then there are words that truly require mastery before we enter the first grade.

4–HELP (Without Humiliation)–There comes a time when love takes on vocabulary distinctions such as the word "Help," a word which every child should know to say and know that every other child in the world needs to learn as well. What is ethics but the fine-tuned study of how to ask for and render aid in relation to others? What is our duty to neighbor and to God and to the person in line with us at the cafeteria at lunch time, and how do we come to the aid of others and ask for aid for ourselves? And how do we ask for and give it without humiliation? Ah, yes, "Help," a fine word worthy of mastery by the time we enter into the first grade.

5–*WAIT*–And there is another like unto Help, which is Wait. To avoid frustration and immense mental anguish, one learns to wait well. If not, there is bitter gnashing of teeth and wailing at the moon. There's waiting for the light to turn green, and waiting for recess, and waiting for church to be over, and waiting for Christmas, and waiting for J.K. Rowling to release her next Harry Potter book, and waiting to be chosen for a part in the school play, and waiting for grades to come out, and waiting in line at the roller-coaster and, when religious sensibilities are primed and keened and made ready, "Waiting for the Lord." Yes, we'd better teach (and learn ourselves as we are teaching) this all important crucial word of social cohesion and sensible daily living.

6–*WELCOME*–And along with Help and Wait, we better teach and learn better ourselves the word, Welcome. Welcome, as in a term of courtesy, "You're Welcome," after someone conveys their thanks. Or more than a cute doormat convention, we say the word "Welcome," to show ourselves not to be doormats, but doorways into relationship. "You're welcome here," the church yearns to say, needs to say, wants to say, even when it's a hard and frightening for some folks to say. "You're Welcome," says the table and the cross and, when we're at our best, each one of us in the face of any stranger. "Welcome." Definitely one of the twelve words we want every child to learn by the time they are twelve years old.

7–*FORGIVE*–From early on our children know this next word, for it trips off their tongues when they recite the Lord's Prayer every time they are in worship. Beyond conquering the enunciation of this word, they need to be grasped by the implanting of its meaning in their hearts as they progress in faith. This is an ultimate human-divine connection word. This is the grounding of reconciliation, no matter how young or old you are. This is the glue of every good marriage. This is the pattern for all friendships which grow and mature over time. This is the essence of what Jesus came to show the world and what we have to accept and absorb in order to become like him.

8–THANKS–I suspect some may have thought I should offer this word a little earlier in the list. But it really belongs here because it's such a hard word to get right. We learn it as a matter of habit. It's certainly one of the "green-light" words we understand about the social dimensions of life. You can't visit another person's home, and eat at their table and get up to go outside or away or and play–without saying this magic word. But it's more than a mere pronouncement of politeness. It's the essence of intimate relationship–with God and with others. No experience of any kind is complete with its intonation. No human bond is strong until Thanks can be expressed. We say in church "Thanks be to God," not merely as rote repetition but as one of the premier ways we can relate to our Maker and Keeper, the Unmoved Mover, the First Cause. The one who made the dawn and allows the dusk. The one who inspires us when we are at our best and comforts us when we are at our worst. This is the word that is best at the beginning of the day when the cocoon of sleep is broken and this is the word that is most appropriate when we are saying our evening prayers. This is a premier reason for our weekly worship gatherings and an ultimate word we say when we say good-bye to a loved one who has died. Thanks and Thanks be to God and Thank You. There is no ending to the times we can say this word.

9–JOY–But beyond the thanks let us not forget to impart the simple, three-letter word Joy. Better than happiness which is too fleeting. Better than pleasure which is too shallow. Better than giddiness that runs out when we run out of breath. Joy is the reason we human beings were made. Joy is our spiritual DNA, though too few people really know this truth and too many people learn it way too late and some not at all. To enjoy is what we were created to do with this startling, breathtakingly beautiful life we live in this wondrous world. Even in the hardest, toughest of circumstances. Especially in the hardest, toughest of circumstances.

*10–ENOUGH–*And who wouldn't be joyful if we master the only other two-syllable word in this list? Enough. This is what we need to learn from an early age. That there is enough. That God is a God of abundance and we need not horde resources or supplies or food. Enough for siblings to share, and for the world to share. Enough–at least enough of anything that finally matters–for all to share. And not only that we have enough. But that we *are* enough, as God has made us in our cantankerous uniqueness. Plenty enough, if we would only accept ourselves as we are, or as Paul Tillich wonderfully describes it, *"to accept that we are accepted."* Enough already. Enough indeed!

*11–WOW!–*And when we master Enough, and truly Enjoy life and are quick to say our Thanks, there comes a time when our children should know how to say a word that goes beyond petition or gratitude and comes close to the elemental way of relating to God.

Donald McCullough recalls how Harry Truman would take is morning walk every day, many times with his friend, Pastor Thomas Melton, through the neighborhood of independence. The daily trek would bring them by a gigantic ginkgo tree, one of the more impressive large trees in Independence. Each time, Truman would walk over to the tree, and then speak to it. After Truman's death, someone inquired of Melton about just what Harry would had said to the tree. "He would say, 'You're doing a good job!'" In his own way, Truman was expressing his own brand of awe and praise to creation.[1]

Wow! At music. And Wow at the sight of grandmother and grandfather and Wow at the sight of candles in this sanctuary on Christmas Eve. And wow at the sight of a baby, and...and...-and Wow at it all.

Which brings us to the final of the dozen words which our children should know before they are twelve years old.

12–GOOD!–This is one of the oldest words in the treasure chest of language's holy words. This is the word that is not only good in and of itself, but it's even better than words like "right" or "superior" or certainly better than "correct."

This is the rod that we want our children to grow into. This is the word that we want them to pass along to others, to their children, and to their children's children. This is the word that God spoke from the beginning of time, before words like justice or power, or righteousness, or any other of the pinnacle of polysyllabic words that are important. This simple, one-syllable word is so important.

One of Community's great elders, Rosetta Gensler, knows the power of this word better than most people I've ever met. "Good,"she says, at the conclusion of a business meeting. "Good," she utters, when the meal is finished and a sweet swelling of satisfaction infuses her being. "Good," she pronounces, when a musical number thrills her soul, and her body even, down to her piano-playing fingers. "This is good," she has remarked, at one meeting or worship service or discussion group gathering or Bible study after another. God, like the Almighty said when He walked among the plants and animals under the beam of the sun and the glow of the moon and all the morning stars sang together at Eden's dawning. "Good" and "Very

Good," when he shared the company of his divinely imaged creatures, humanity, you and me. Good, Good, Good–the mere pronouncing of it performs its meaning. It seems almost to make things holy, which is exactly what we want to teach to our children.

1–YES; 2–NO; 3–LOVE; 4–HELP (Without Humiliation); 5–WAIT; 6–WELCOME; 7–FORGIVE; 8–THANKS; 9–JOY; 10–-ENOUGH; 11–WOW!; 12–GOOD!

If our children will learn these words, and learn them well, then they will not only act wisely, they will be wise indeed. Which is the best which the author of the book of the Proverbs and we keeper of proverbs could ever hope for. Let it be SO. AMEN.

Notes

1 Thanks to Thomas Long for a reminder of this passage in his Testimony.

15

How to Negate Negativity

Text: Ephesians 4:25, 31-32

The romantic and comical words of Cole Porter's old standard rings ever truer these days.

"You say tomāto, I say tomâto,
You say potāto, I say potâto.
Tomāto, tomâto,
Potāto, potâto,
Let's call the whole thing off!"

Only now, these cute and cuddly words are prickly and potentially violent. These sorts of words can be said and are said in the midst of the most contentious, divisive, rancorous, adversarial, oppositional, and negative culture known to humanity. Look and behold what we have wrought:

- All children born since the height of the baby boom, have seen or will see more than 50,000 killings before graduation from high school, nearly all (but not all of them, frighteningly!) from viewing television.
- Our newspapers do not give much press ink for good news, but rather focus on the burgeoning body count or murder

rate. (Just two years ago, the *Kansas City Star,* as well as most of the local television stations were grievously guilty of paying inordinate attention to the rise in Kansas City's murder rate, especially as it related to our children being killed, and not much attention at all to any of the good things caused by the citizenry of our communities.

- We greet each other, with seemingly niceties and funny sayings, but they betray a downward cast in our spirits. I heard one such greeting just this past week, as a clergy colleague, when asked how he was doing, sardonically greeted a group of us in an elevator with the salutation, *"Oh pretty bad, but tomorrow is going to be worse."*

In fact, we could say that the United States of America is consumed with "negativity." In Texas, when someone has an extremely bad case of cancer, the colloquial way of describing the person's condition is to say he or she is "eaten up with the big C." We might easily say, if providing a diagnosis of the current culture, America is eaten up with negativity. From talk-radio call-in shows to the slamming, jamming, bashing, trash-talking, so-called interview television programs, we have become eaten up with negativity. The dissension and contrariness of our culture have nearly become our sole societal diet, infusing us with a deadly dosage of vitamin "N"–negativity.

Even the most positive among us, from time to time, have become negative in their own fashion. (I must admit and observe that the title of this sermon smacks a bit negatively–*"How to* **negate** *negativity."* But I'm in good company.) Consider the great one, Albert Einstein, who could see a positive "charge" in nearly every encounter with reality–and thus could admonish us to know a great positive truism that "imagination is more important than knowledge"–had his negative take on things. When Einstein saw the Pacific Ocean for the first time, he literally wept, it is reported, he was so overwhelmed "at seeing all that energy going to waste."

Well, what do we do about all this negativity? How do we handle the pessimism, skepticism, and cynicism which increasingly plague our time?

We can take a clear clue from Ephesians and its positive counsel about **prohibitions** and **prescriptions.**

Prohibitions

Now, the first of the prohibitions mentioned in this Ephesians passage is fundamental. It is the bedrock for the rest of the remedy to negativity...

I. Putting Away All Falsehood

Which means to deal with reality as it presents itself to us, without delusion and without denial. A lot of us golfers are into delusion and denial. Some golfers are convinced that he or she is a Nancy Lopez or an Arnold Palmer or a Ben Crenshaw. And they become exceedingly frustrated by their inability to perform like a professional. I am reminded, by contrast, of the man who couldn't hit a straight golf shot to save his life. Yet, he always had a smile on his face. If he knocked a "duck hook" to the left or a "banana slice" to the right, he always was able to say, *"Well, I don't mind where I hit my ball. I'm just glad to find the ball and myself on the right side of the grass."*

Putting away all falsehood also means that we deal realistically with our own limitations and stop our worrying. Too often we are down-in-the-dumps because of worry and fret. Erma Bombeck reminds us of how overly much we all worry. She wrote comically but cunningly about the subject:

I've always worried a lot and frankly I'm good at it.

I worry about introducing people and going blank when I get to my mother.

I worry about a shortage of ball bearings; a snake coming up through the kitchen drain.

I worry about the world ending at midnight and getting stuck with three hours on a twenty-four hour cold capsule.

I worry about getting into the Guiness Book of World Records under "Pregnancy: Oldest Recorded Birth."

I worry what the dog thinks when he sees me coming out of the shower...

I worry about salesladies following me into the fitting room, oil slicks, and Carol Channing going bald.

I worry about scientists discovering someday that lettuce has been fattening all along.[1]

You can also overcome the negativity of your circumstances, the Ephesians passage suggests, secondly, if you will...

II. Put Away from You All Bitterness and...

Did you hear the string of negativities listed in the passage when it was first read this morning. "*Put away from you all bitterness and wrath and anger and wrangling and slander, together with all malice...*" Whew! Where do we begin with such an avalanche of vileness? Surely we can begin to overcome such low and loathsome negativities by raising our expectations.

I like what Carl Boyd, the founder and creator of *The Art of Positive Teaching* here in Kansas City, has to say about maintaining a positive posture toward existence and how it can help us ascend to great heights of new achievement. The motto for his positively-oriented teaching is: "*No one rises to low expectations!*" And he's right, as you know. Lower your expectations, and you'll soon arrive at lower achievements. But raise those expectations, and you'll quickly discover that your attainments also rise.

Carl tells the wonderful story of Mrs. Dougherty, a teacher in a Miami, Florida, junior high school. One year, she was assigned what all her colleague teachers and other educators elsewhere would call "that class." "That class" was composed of students who usually had one tennis shoe directed toward the principal's office for disciplinary purposes and the other pointed toward the nearest restroom or exit door. "That class" was made up of "those students"–the least desirable, most troublesome students. "That class."

Well, Mrs. Dougherty worried about preparing for her new class. A certain policy disallowed her from seeing the confidential files of her students. She was particularly interested in the part of her students files indicating their IQ scores. If she was going to have to pull hard duty with "that class," she thought she should have as much advantage as she could muster before they arrived for the first day of class. Finally, she went to inquire of the principal if, just this once, she might abrogate the prohibition against seeing the files and have a peek. After all, she reasoned, as the principal clearly knew, she was going to be in charge of "that class." The principal wasn't in, so she waited. Surprisingly, she spied her class' file right on the principal's desk. So she had a look. Lo and behold, she was startled at what she discovered! In the list of her class' students was a name and then a number, 134. Another student's name, and a 128. Another student's name, and a 140. All in all, numbers ranged from 126 to 142. "My, my," Mrs. Dougherty thought to herself, "this puts a whole new light on things!" Now, was she ever ready for the first day of class!

As soon as the students arrived, Mrs. Dougherty lit into them. "Now," she admonished her new charges, "I know something about you that didn't know I knew. And I'm not going to tell you what I know, but I *am* going to set the following rules. From now on, you will sit up in your seats. Whenever I ask for an answer to a particular problem or area of discussion, I want to see 80 percent of your hands in the air in response. And of those hands in the air, 80 per cent of those will have the right answer. From now on, you will speak in clear sentences, and you will be courteous. From here on out, all homework assignments will be handed in neatly done, with good penmanship, on clean paper, on the corner of my desk and on time, not a second after the deadline. Everyone got that?"

Mrs. Dougherty's high, high expectations began to have immediate results. Eventually, the whole faculty of the school and its good leader, the principal, noticed as well. During one of the breaks between classes, the principal dropped by Mrs. Dougherty's class room to discuss the amazing change in her students' achievement rate. "Everybody's talking about what you've accomplished, Mrs. Dougherty. It's truly amazing! How did you do it?" In reply, Mrs. Dougherty then mustered up her courage and confessed her violation pertaining to the student's confidential information. "Well," he said, much to her surprise, "I want to commend you for your resourcefulness. You deserve extremely high praise for raising the expectations of your students. You've tapped into their potential with daring and effectiveness, and I commend you." Mrs. Dougherty was dumbfounded! Was he letting her get away with such a brazen violation of policy. "And you're not mad?" she queried. "No, as I've already said, I admire your resourcefulness." And then he spoke over his shoulder on his way out of the classroom, "Besides, those weren't IQ scores you saw." "What?!" she exclaimed. "They weren't?! Then what were they?" "Those were your students' locker numbers right outside your classroom, locker numbers 128 through 142."[2]

But it's not enough to put *away* our negativities. Prohibitions inspiring us to "put away" that which would harm the human community and the life of faith are indeed necessary and right. But we must put *on* a positive posture.

Prescriptions

The writer to the Ephesians knew this, so our text includes three antidotes for our negative sicknesses. The first gentle **prescription** reminds us to...

I. Be Kind to One Another

Now, being kind to one another entails looking up. Maya Angelou reminds us...

Lift up your eyes
Upon this day breaking for you.
Give birth again
To the dream

...Lift up you hearts
Each new hour holds new chances
For a new beginning.
Do not be wedded forever
To fear, yoked eternally
To brutishness.[3]

In order to lift up our eyes and our hearts in kindness, we need good examples. And when you have good examples in kindness, kindness shines through you in everything you do. Last December, Crystal Detmer taught two ministers what gentle kindness is all about and what good teachers she has had all along.

On the night of the dedication of our wondrous "Steeple of Light," Crystal had been tapped as the member of our congregation–quite literally, at the age of eight, a congregant of "the church of the future"–for the duty of turning on the actual switch which would "light up" the steeple's electrical apparatus. But when the time came for Crystal to do her duty, she demurred. In fact, she protested. Instead of doing as she had agreed to do, she wanted to share the responsibility of the "light-up" with her friend. Richard Woodard, our associate pastor, who was over-all in-charge of the arrangements on the rooftop where the "light-up" would occur, was emphatic, "No, Crystal, *you* are to do the switching on! This is for the sake of history! Years from now, you'll be able to tell your children that *you* were the first one to officially turn on Community's "Steeple of Light"! Now, come on!" But Crystal didn't care about some future historic posterity. All she wanted to do was gently, kindly share the shining moment with her friend! Where did Crystal get that sort of kindness? How did she know, better than Richard or I or any of the rest of us, what are the really important priorities in human relations? I'll tell you. Bob and Beth, her grandparents who have raised her with gentleness and care and kindness, *they* are the ones who taught Crystal be so stubbornly, persistently, and faithfully kind.

Now, the second prescription is similar to the first, but it contains dynamic differences, too. The Ephesians passage would have us know that we are called to...

II. Be Tenderhearted

Being tenderhearted, I want to suggest to you today, is ultimately determined by how much we are willing to allow our hearts to become filled with the tender mercy of God's powerful and yet humbling presence.

Lee Atwater was once known as a brutal, consummate political strategist and hardball Republican Committee chair. Then he had a repentant and renewing revolution in his life, became a Christian. Struggling with brain cancer, he advocated for radical change in national politics, because, as he described the US, our nation had a "tumor on its soul." In the end, he made an astonishing challenge to us all:

"I acquired more [wealth, power, and prestige] than most," he

said. "But you can acquire all you want, and still feel empty. It took a deadly illness to put me eye to eye with that truth, but it is a truth that the country, caught up in its ruthless ambitions and moral decay, can learn on my dime. [Leaders] speak to the spiritual vacuum at the heart of American society... What is missing in society is what was missing in me: a little heart."[4]

In order to become tenderhearted allow me to urge you to become as Anne Lamott eventually became, extraordinarily, fundamentally **open to the surprising, serendipitous grace of God,** In her wonderful memoir of her son Sam's first year of life, Anne Lamott, a single mother who successfully overcame dual addictions to cocaine and alcohol, describe's how grace has worked in her life, and, more importantly, in her heart. Lamott recalls...

"Last night I decided that it is totally nuts to believe in Christ... Then something truly amazing happened. A man from church showed up at our front door, smiling and waving to me and Sam, and I went to let him in. He is a white man named Gordon, fiftyish, married to our associate pastor, and after exchanging pleasantries he said, 'Margaret and I wanted to do something for you and the baby. So what I want to ask is, What if a fairy appeared on your doorstep and said that he or she would do any favor for you at all, anything you wanted around the house that you felt too exhausted to do by yourself and too ashamed to ask anyone else to help you with?'

"'I can't even say,' I said. 'It's too horrible.'

"But finally he convinced me to tell him, and I said it would be to clean the bathroom, and he ended up spending an hour scrubbing the bathtub and toilet and sink with Ajax and lots of hot water. I sat on the couch while he worked, watching TV, feeling vaguely guilty and nursing Sam to sleep. But it

made me feel sure of Christ again, of that kind of love. This, a man scrubbing a new mother's bathtub, is what Jesus means to me. As Bill Rankin, my priest friend, once said, spare *me the earnest Christians.*"[5]

But let us not forget the absolutely crucial element highlighted by this passage from Ephesians, namely that of...

III. Forgiving One Another

It almost always comes down to one form of forgiveness or another. Forgiveness is an ultimate weapon in the battle against negativity, forgiveness of oneself and forgiveness of one another. Our mistakes confuse us about issues of ultimate worth. We become accusing toward others and incriminating toward ourselves. Then we lose all perspective and forget the positive possibilities for change and transformation latent within humanity's being. It is important to recall the power of God's forgiving, transforming love.

Ernest T. Campbell, former Senior Minister of Riverside Church in New York City reminds us that God is a "Supreme Being of Second Chances."

"'*Once to every man and nation [comes the moment to decide],' we sing. But people and civilizations get many more chances than one. If the church is built on Peter it is built on the second chance. Life is not like a spelling bee. One miss and you are out.*"[6]

Oh, yes the church of Jesus Christ is absolutely, incontrovertibly a place and a people where second chances are offered freely and gladly to any and all who will receive them.

Conclusion

Ten days or so ago, I went to church at the Grand Emporium Bar and Grill, right down on Main Street, between 39th and 38th streets. Yes, you heard right, church. I was there to hear the Five Blind Boys of Alabama. The Five Blind Boys are a legendary gospel group, led by the incomparable voice of Clarence Fountain. Now, to be very frank, I had never been that close to any blind performer. Oh, I had seen Ray Charles and Stevie Wonder on television, but I had never actually been that intimately close to any blind performer on any stage in person. It was a transformative experience. Clarence Fountain, with his incredible range (from a high tenor falsetto to the depths of all bass notes) and his sassy, emphatic, grace-filled style, charmed and challenged and changed me. And it was all for the better. As the old country saying goes, "We really had church!" Among the tinkling of cocktail glasses and the fog of the smoke lilting over countless ash trays, Clarence and his musically magical, blind cohorts pierced through to our hearts with a bonafide gospel message. Here were the Five Blind Boys, singing... *"Oh, I ain't what I oughta be, and I ain't what I'm gonna be, 'cause God's given me a second chance."* Surely this was manifestly true. In their lyrical, harmonious presentations and their very lives, an enraptured audience heard how God could indeed take anybody, no matter how ravaged by any sort of negativity (including the ravaging of blindness) and transform them into an amazing vessel for grace. Oh yes, I believe we could all sing a verse or two of that great gospel refrain: *"Oh, I ain't what I oughta be, and I ain't what I'm gonna be, 'cause God's given me a second chance."*

The letter to the Ephesians gives us clear guidance for a new way of life which overcomes the negativities of our world with positive passions, helpful hopes, and strong loves, if we will: [1] put away falsehoods; [2] put away all bitterness (and other gruesome forms of negativity); and, more importantly and positively, if we will [1] be kind to one another; [2] be tender-hearted; and [3] forgive one another. Could there be any better present to offer on Mother's Day than the faith-filled overcoming of the destructiveness of negativity? AMEN.

Notes

1 quoted in Max Lucado's *He Still Moves Stones*, 1993, p. 59

2 Carl Boyd, "No One Rises to Low Expectations," conference address given at the *"Hear Their Cries: A Faith Community Response to Child Abuse"* at the University of Missouri–Kansas City, May 10, 1995

3 Maya Angelou, *On the Pulse of Morning*, New York: Random House, 1993)

4 "Missing a Little Heart," in *"Sweet's Cafe,"* Vol. 1, No. 2, February, 1995, p. 5

5 Anne Lamott, *Operating Instructions: A Journal of My Son's First Year*, 1993, pp. 69-70

6 from *Campbell's Notebook*

16

Architecture of the Spirit

Text: Ephesians 3:17-18

In China, in ancient times, the feet of young girls were bound and restricted so as to mold and form them in certain shapes and patterns. Small feet were prized in that culture, so painful bindings were put on the feet of little girls to keep their little feet just that, little. (God only knows how much painful twisting-contorting-warping such practices caused, not only on the feet of Chinese women but in their spirits and personalities down through the years!)

Mickey Mantle's father gave his baby new son the name of his favorite baseball catcher of all time, Mickey Cochrane. Then as he watched his son growing up in Oklahoma – and especially as he tutored him early on in the wondrous art of playing baseball – he required Mickey to bat from both sides of the plate. Day by day, game by game, year after year, Mickey was made to bat first from the left side of the plate (against all right-handed pitchers) and then from the right side of the plate (against all left-handed pitchers). Years later, when Mickey Mantle had become the greatest switch-hitter in the history of the beloved game and was accorded baseball's highest honor, induction into the Hall of Fame in Cooperstown, New York, Mickey turned the tribute toward his father who had "made" him into the star he became.

And, please note, in our front yard, right by our driveway stands the oldest redbud tree existent in all of Kansas City. At first, a few years ago, I wanted to cut it down, seeing as how it was getting so old and gnarled, far more gruesome-looking, as redbud trees go, than it should have looked. I thought, "This tree's time has come. Get ready for the pencil factory!" But Priscilla wouldn't have it. She was convinced that it could go on forever. Then, I thought I would at least cut off the redbud tree's low hanging limb that covers the space of about twenty running feet. "My goodness," I thought again to myself, "this is unsightly. So much trouble, really doubly ugly, if you ask me, and besides, it's a royal pain in my tennis shoes every time I have to mow the grass under-and-around that blasted redbud limb. It's time for at least that low-slung awkward tree limb to get ready for the pencil factory!" But, once, more, Priscilla prevailed. Instead of felling the ancient, rotting giant toothpick, she asked me to trim it, shape it just so, so as to enhance the sweeping, leafy spray of that ugly limb!

Now, the trick to this message is to discern the thread of thematic continuity woven into each of these illustrations. I mention these examples to trace that thread which is a dramatic truth about our lives: *all life is shaped, formed or fashioned.* Random molding is an impossibility. How something looks today was shaped by a form or a force yesterday. How we act in today's moment had a precedent of some sort or another in a previous moment. The way we walk, the manner of our talk, the lilt in our laughter, the tilt of our heads–all these were influenced, in major ways and minor ways, by the walk and the talk, the lilt and the tilt of others.

Sociologists and anthropologists of a certain stripe would exclaim with smiling satisfaction: "Ah, yes, you've finally got it–Determinism! You've finally grasped the ultimate genius of this crucial notion! Touché for you!" But, no, I am *not* here to verify a deterministic view of human life. In my opinion, determinism is–as Emerson once said about the subject of consistency–*"the hobgoblin of little minds."*

Rather, I am here to affirm, with you, the fact that there is a shaping of human life. Ah, what good clichés we have for affirming this obvious reality!

- *"What goes around comes around!"*
- *"The hand that rocks the cradle rules the world."*

And do not forget Mark Twain's old bromide:

- *"Things are more like they are today than they ever have been before."*

Now, just as there is no getting around the shaping of human life, we need to acknowledge and understand anew that there is an "architecture for the spirit."

By "architecture" I don't mean just the wondrous configurations we naturally link with religious experience.

- the tall spire reaching to a heavenly beyond
- the "little brown church in the dale" (which really turned out to be a white wooden frame church atop of lowly hill)
- the auditory "architecture" of peeling church bells
- an arrangement of church pews in rows & aisles
- a cruciform shape of a church nave, with Christ's communion table in the center, the church choir in the back, aisles of worshipers out in front and two side sections (the "crossbeams" of the cruciform) for other worshipers.

- Or – and this one is a natural focus for us – the sight of our own church's "Steeple of Lights" with its lightbeams searing through the night-time sky, ever upward, infinitely onward, inspiring all onlookers, believers and agnostics alike, reminding them of an ascending Truth that towers over all human machinations.

No, rather, when I refer to the "architecture for the spirit," I mean to highlight the great, yet simple metaphorical description which the New Testament letter to the Ephesian Christians emphasizes: *"...that you, being rooted and grounded in love, may have the power to comprehend, with all the saints, what is the breadth and length and height and depth, and to know the love of Christ...the fullness of God"* (Eph. 3:17-18).

I. Breadth

The-love-of-Christ/the-fullness-of-God has dramatic dimensions. And the first of these striking dimensions is *breadth*. The writer to the church at Ephesus wanted the readers of the letter to look beyond the parameters of their own meager experiences there in the Mediterranean world. The writer wanted any and all Christians, I believe, to see that the breadth (the broadness) of their faith would determine how much their faith could grow and develop.

Some Christians believe that their faith is just as broad as it needs to be, that they've arrived, that their baptisms were the destination points for their spiritual journey and not the launching pads. Some folks confuse their particular tree of belief for the whole forest of faith, and thus their faith is dwarfed, truncated, and, upon occasion, virtually snuffed out.

I have known folks in churches nearly everywhere who regarded themselves as unworthy of an elder's position, because they had not "achieved" a righteous-enough status.

Then there are other Christians who see a broadening vista,

ever expanding before them, calling them forward and out of their own little cubbyholes and bailiwicks. When a Christian is broadened like this along their spiritual journey, an architecture of breadth is challenging and changing them for the better. And we all need such challenge and change. This facet of the breadth of the love of Christ is an absolutely necessary feature for an appropriate "architecture for the spirit."

Oliver Sacks, the celebrated scientist made famous by Robin Williams in the movie "Awakenings," has given us new understanding of how we can broaden our grasp of the possibilities of life, by showing us how some very unlikely candidates have broadened their existence. In his new book *An Anthropologist on Mars,* Sacks speaks of how folks normally regarded as sick have broadened their lives through sheer, mysterious grace. *"Sickness implies a contraction of life, but such contractions do not have to occur."* Sack's patients *"reach out to life–and not only despite their conditions, but often because of them, and even with their aid."*[1] The seven patients whose "narratives of nature" make up Sack's powerful and imaginative book on the mind, include: a color-blind painter; a young prodigy who is autistically rigid except for his artwork; a master brain surgeon with Tourette's Syndrome; and perhaps, most profoundly, the autistic Temple Grandin, who has managed to overcome her nature so thoroughly that she wrote her own book. Oliver Sacks spends time with each of them and writes about them with an empathy that touches your heart.

And how does Sacks manage to touch our hearts? Sacks reminds us of our very own possibilities for broadening. We are called (and challenged) by the example of Sack's seven friendly souls to broaden our own journeys, to broaden our faith, to expand our reach toward the expanse of God's great world within us and outside of us. Such broadening is an invitation not only for us but for all who would follow down the broad path of Jesus' way.

II. Length

The way of the carpenter from Nazareth is not only broad; it is also long. By *length*, I believe the writer to the Christians in Ephesus was meaning to highlight the length of God's love for all of creation.

But, wait, let's face it! Modern Americans can hardly fathom the length of God's love.

Despite the psychotherapists and self-help gurus among us clamoring for us all to slow down, we abide, without too much resistance, in a hurry-up world. (Witness the continuing rise of heart disease and stroke casualties nearly everywhere in the United States.)

Despite the ever-lengthening of our physical longevity, most people claim that there seems to be less and less time for fewer and fewer tasks.

And though we strike again and again the carillon signal to care for our children with "quantity time" and not just so-called "quality time," there seems to be an ever-shrinking stretch of time available for any of us to spend with anybody. (Did you hear the National Public Radio declaration a few months ago that some people must get in their cars to have a conversation with their spouse, there's so little time for them to converse in their kitchens or living rooms?!?!?)

As this passage in Ephesians reminds us, we are called to lengthen our lives, our faith, our souls by remembering *God's* long, long, long, long love for us. The length dimension of the "architecture for the spirit" is God's long love for every one of us.

In reflecting on John 3:16–"For God so loved the world that he gave his only Son, that whoever believes in him should not perish but have eternal life"–award-winning author Reynolds Price describes the gospel of John as containing "the sentence that humanity craves from stories–'The Maker of all things loves and wants me.'"[2]

The love of God is indeed the length dimension in the "architecture for the spirit." But there is still more. Apart from the breadth dimension to this metaphorical "architecture for the spirit," and different from the length dimension of it, there is something even more distinctive and impressive, and here we can use the third term listed in the Ephesian letter...

III. Height

Clearly, faith has a *height* dimension. This is why we worship, to reach upward toward the God who made us, redeems us, and sustains us.

For as long as I can recall, the *"up"* dimension has always been figural for me and for nearly every Christian person I know. Consider the following...

- We speak of God being *"up there."*
- We send our prayers *"upward."*
- Some Christians sing or pray with their hands lifted in an *"upturned"* posture.
- When we speak of the saints who have gone on before us, we regularly talk about them being *"up* in heaven."
- Our liturgies taken from Scripture consistently shout out the clarion call to "Lift *up* your head, O gates!"
- When we are outside and some reference is made concerning the weather or the appearance of the sky or the feel of the wind, we will turn our gazes *"upward"* and speak about what God has done meteorologically.
- We hope and pray and trust that our faith will provide us a way by which we not only can keep our spirits *"up"* but live with an *"upward"* tilt to our walking and "upward"

angle in our looking and an *"upward,"* positive stance in our basic attitude toward existence.

But the upward pull of the "architecture for the spirit" doesn't have to do just with the way we talk about God. It also has to do with the way we orient ourselves toward others and ourselves.

I like how Maya Angelou orients herself in her strong poem *"And Still I Rise."*

You may shoot me with your words,
You may cut me with your eyes,
You may kill me with your hatefulness,
But still, like air, I rise.

Out of the huts of history's shame
I rise
Up from a past that's rooted in pain
I rise
I'm a black ocean, leaping and wide,
Welling and swelling I bear in the tide.

Leaving behind nights of terror and fear
I rise
Into a daybreak that's wondrously clear
I rise
Bringing the gifts that my ancestors gave,
I am the dream and the hope of the slave.
I rise,
I rise,
I rise.[3]

I believe what Maya Angelou was getting at had to do with the honor she intended to pay to her forebears and to the integrity of her own life.

There is another kind of honor that is due to God. I learned about this sort of honoring several years ago while participating in the Christmas Eve activities of the Thomas Chapel Disciples congregation in New Haven, Connecticut. During this particular worship service, a soon-to-become-familiar phrase was used whenever anyone addressed the congregation. Before the announcements. At the time for prayer requests. At the occasion of the offering. Before preaching. When they introduced a special choral anthem. It was always the same:

"Giving honor to God and giving honor to all the brothers and sisters here today..."

What happened in me whenever that phrase was uttered was a soaring of the spirit. It infused everybody, really, with an upward lilt to our worship. "Giving honor to God..." Isn't that what we are all about here at Community Christian Church? Isn't that what any church worthy of the name is all about? And isn't it usually the case, that we can more readily honor our brothers and sisters with respect once we've honored God with worship?

Honor is the height dimension in an appropriate "architecture for the spirit." And, yet, there is another, intriguing, absolutely essential dimension that defies our normal three-dimensional schemes. That dimension is...

IV. Depth

Now, this *"depth"* referred to in the Ephesian letter is not merely the other end of height, although it would be natural for us to think of it so. No, this "depth" dimension goes beyond our usual three-dimensional world, in a similar way that the microscopic (normally unseen) world goes beyond the three-dimensionality of our physical existence. There is, in other words, a depth to our spiritual journey that is the real gist of any grace-filled life. There is a kind of "D-N-A" in our spiritual selves. And that "D-N-A" is the "divine, natural attribute" within us and among us. And what is that "D-N-A"? It is simply God's caring devotion to creation. I repeat, for those of us who are part of the Body of Christ, the depth dimension of spiritual life is the "divine, natural attribute" of God's caring devotion.

To craft or fashion or shape or form or construct or mold or pattern or make our lives into anything approaching a righteous character or a Godly manner, we have to tap into the deep, deep creativity of God's character and that character is constituted completely in caring devotion.

The deep, caring devotion of God is what keeps us coming back to church; it puts us back together when we're broken and sends us into a broken world in need of healing.

The deep, caring devotion of God is what picks us up when we think we are defeated and applies holy finishing touches when we're sure we'll die uncompleted.

The deep, caring devotion of God is the foundation for forgiveness between each of us and God and among all of us in the human community.

The deep, caring devotion of God is what forms us into caring parents and loving friends, into devoted members of the church and willing volunteers in civic organizations.

The deep, caring devotion of God–the divine, natural attribute–is deep, deep, deep; it's as deep as, no *deeper* than anything else in all the world! As the apostle Paul put it to the Christians in Rome (according to a contemporary, vernacular translation):

For I am rock-solid sure that
neither the threat of death,
nor the struggles of life,
nor the dreams of angelic rescue,
nor the domination of earthly rulers,
nor things happening now,
nor things unforeseen in the future,
nor the power beyond our regular reckoning,
nor the height of folly,

nor the depth of despair,
nor anything else in the totality of the cosmos,
will ever be able to cut us off
from God's deep abiding caring devotion
in Christ Jesus our Lord.[4]

When we understand the "architecture for the spirit" and understand such architecture as crucial for the development of our faith, we will know with a fresh sensitivity and a new awareness the power and veracity of what the ol' rascal Martin Luther believed:

"This life is not righteousness but growth in righteousness, not health but healing, not being but becoming, not rest but exercise. We are not yet what we shall be, but we are growing toward it. The process is not yet finished, but it is going on. This is not the end, but it is the road."[5]

And then we will know that the "architecture for the spirit" is not the final building of God's realm of love and justice. But it is the blueprint...it is the plan...it is the way, the truth and the life. In the name of that One whom we proclaim as "the way, the truth and the life," Jesus Christ, AMEN.

Notes

1 Oliver Sacks, *An Anthropologist on Mars*, 1995, pp. xviii.
2 Reynolds Price, *"The Gospel of John,"* in *Testament*, 1992.
3 Maya Angelou, *The Complete Collected Poems of Maya Angelou*, 1994, pp. 163-164.
4 My paraphrase translation of Romans 8:38-39.
5 Martin Luther, quoted in Richard Lischer's *The Preacher King: Martin Luther King, Jr., and the Word that Moved America*, 1995, p. 233.

17

Things I Know Now That I Wish Knew Then

Institute of Spirituality & Health
Shawnee Mission Medical Center

There are things we wish we knew when we begin starting out on a venture, or a profession, or a relationship, or a project. We wish we had a glimpse or a hint or a glimmer of the dangers and challenges that lie ahead. We wish we had some kind of heads-up about what to watch out for in the adjudicating of important matters of life, in the enactment of a meaningful life.

So it is with all of us who, I believe, have been blessed with the occasions and opportunities of being of use in relation to people in the extremis moments of their lives, when health is at issue, and especially at the end-of-life.

There are some things I know now—as a pastor and a preacher—that I wish I had known then. I wouldn't have so many hard miles in my soul and body, and, I believe, I would have, could have been more effective as a minister.

I wish I had known...

- My older peers weren't as stuffy and un-cool as I thought they were.

- How...well...“funereal” (i.e. dead!) some funeral music can be.
- How much a meal – the breaking of bread – can be a sacrament.
- How life-extending machinery would revolutionize the whole essence of end-of-life care.
- How much doctors and nurses need pastoral care in the middle of their work.
- How important it is for clergy to take time away after a funeral.
- How necessary it is to care-givers in end-of-life situations – clergy-chaplains, et al. – to take ample time for spiritual retreats.
- How little musicians and organists get paid for their essential participation in funeral services.
- That every minister needs a priest or rabbi and every priest needs a minister or rabbi and every rabbi needs a priest or minister.
- How very difficult and ultimately rewarding interfaith work is.
- I wish I had known that we clergy have more power than we know. Along with physicians, nurses, and chaplains, we clergy have immense capacities to educate, to illuminate, to enlighten our peers in other professions. Not only do we have the capacity to do so, we have a duty to do so. Too often clergy are relegated to what I call “the afterwards role” – funeral, burial, etc. after all the tough stuff – heroic measures or pain management – has been performed. Too often the work we do during a person’s illness – prayer, visitation, communion, anointing, simple presence – is seen as ancillary (a side-bar action) as adjacent to the central work of the medical professional. If I had known how nec-

essary and impact-laden a clergy's actions are to a congregant's health, I would have pressed earlier and harder for conversation with doctors and nurses and technicians, so that we all might benefit and so that my congregants (and their patients) could receive a more holistic, more effective attention and treatment. And I would have begun, a lot earlier, to invite the entire health care team to the funeral. For the health care and hospital personnel need – spiritually need! – to see their patients deaths not as failures but as completions of an earthly journey.

- I wish I had known then what I know now: a hearty and honestly related expression of ignorance is more welcome and better appreciated than the empty platitudes that sometimes pass for piety. What I mean, straightforwardly, here, is that, before we do any more damage, we ought to quit, back off our half-baked notions of the Divine and the Divine's intention for all of us humans. Too often we clergy act and speak as if we know much more than we actually do, in fact, really know. Rarely have I known, in exact detail, what is truly the will of God. And our people, those souls who have placed their trust in us know this with a consummate clarity. More often that not our members need most to know we are with them in their struggles and they are not alone, that they are being accompanied by God and by you and me, through the last passage toward their completion upon this globe. That they need and deeply hunger for real information and real comfort and tough honesty, rather than some eked-out, trumped-up presumption about what the will of God is in the midst of a death-dealing cancer at the age of 49.
- I wish I had known more science – in college or graduate school – so I wouldn't have had to play catch-up (usually

over some nurse's shoulder)–about blood gasses, blood pressure, and how much blood there is and where it is in the human body. Yes, we all know the sound of rattled breathing when death is fast approaching in the ICU. But I have not until the last eight years known how renal failure occurs and at what point the autonomic takes charge and kicks in within the human creature.

- I would have said "I love you" more often, more directly, more clearly to the members of the congregations I have served. We clergy are occasionally stiff and stuffed-to-the-gills with our own personal dignity when we think that composure and strength are called for. An aloof detachment, a stern countenance, a stuff upper lip in the midst of the dying and death–all these are shames and failures. Conrad Aiken's couplet needs an additional line to make it into a holy trilogy of truths–

  Music I heard with you was more than music,
  bread I broke with you was more than bread.
  Tears I shared with you were sheer sacrament

  We all should be like Jeremiah–free and full in our weeping–with and on behalf of our people.
- I wish I had known then how costly hospital care is and how the press of the costs can psychologically and spiritually oppress those at the end of life and those who remain. I wish I had known just how costly funerals can be and how affordable cremation is and when to suggest one or the other to a family who is strapped financially.
- I wish I had known how personal and pummeled and pulverized and pounded all doctors and nurses are by forces and factors that have nothing to do with the medical arts and sciences in which they were trained and little if anything to do with the rendering of service in which they

perform their duties. I wish I had known that political correctness and what the Bible calls "avarice"(or greed–one of the "major league" seven deadly sins in Catholic tradition) is as much a problem plaguing doctors by those above them as it is for all of us.

- I wish I had known that the emphysema patient still smoking and the cirrhosis patient still drinking and the morbidly obese patient still overeating all signal a family dysfunctionality so wherever a death-wish is being lived out, there's a death-wish script being transmitted to a new generation.
- I wish I had known during the first ten years of my ministerial journey what I have known for the last 10 years–that funeral home directors have an increasingly heavy load of grief-related work on their plates, especially as the culture seems to express an anti-institutional bent when it comes to religion.
- I wish I had known how idolatrous every generation is of their own youth and youthfulness.
- I wish I had known how much we Americans–for at least the last 50 years, but never so rabidly as during the last 15 years– have made an idol of convenience.
- I wish I had known how frequently it will be the case that an estranged, distant relative will intrude in an end-of-life situation with their own narcissistic needs.
- I wish I had known how utterly grace-filled it is to hold the hand of someone who is contemplating their death and then to hold their hand as they are dying, how simply holy it is that their beloved is on one side of them and their rabbi, their pastor, their priest, their imam, is on the other side of them–as they are ushered into the next plane of their existence.

Ash Wednesday Proclamations

18

The Touch

Text: Luke 4:16-21

We Are Here

Each of us is here for a tangle of reasons. Some keep coming back for this "movable feast," year after year, to commence, as you've always commenced the annual Lenten journey of the 40 days between today and Easter's resurrection celebration (excepting the Sundays, of course, which, as you know, are consider "little Easters"). Call it tradition or habit or a "personal rhythm." The motivations in this vein go by many names.

Some us are here, admittedly, are striving–to use the converse of the great phrase of the Bard of Avon–to overcome the long discontent of this too long winter. (I dearly love snow. I suppose growing up in the "Holy Land" of the Rio Grande Valley of Texas afforded precious few instances of exposure to the lacy white grace that now blankets our city. But I'm truly, ultimately, fed-up-to-here tired of it now!) As with the weather so our sojourns as human beings: we have the nagging suspicion, a holy curiosity, that life could be otherwise than it is.

Some of us are also here to make a life-shifting decision, to alter completely the path of our faith journey. Some of those of us gathered here are "sick and tired of being sick and tired" of the way our lives are. Some may consider themselves adrift and feel themselves inept in matters of the Spirit, and thus are looking for a better way. A better way of living, a better way of working, a better way of relating, a better way of worshiping, a better way of praying, a better way, all in all, of being a Christian.

We all of us are here, as well to see about this God-man named Jesus–to see what he's up to and to discern–if at all possible and feasible–if what he's up to–in some mysterious way, in some mysterious fashion–relates to us.

A Scene in Nazareth

There may be no better text in the entirety of the New Testament than Luke 4:16-21 to investigate what Jesus Christ is up to. Did you hear earlier the revolutionary implications, the resounding transformations that this text indicates? In his self-described "job description," Jesus reveals his message, his mission, and his meaning for the world. For the next few weeks we will explore this text in detail to understand its multivalent, multifaceted power–and to relate to the impact it can have on our lives as people of faith.

The scene is clear: Jesus is preaching what in some circles would be described as his "trial sermon" before his hometown synagogue. This is his hometown of Nazareth, where he grew up and participated in the "JYF" ("Jewish Youth Fellowship"). Here, from some anonymous instructor, he learned Hebrew so that he might be able to read scripture one day–this very day–in the context of worship. Here he learned the ritual of his day for proper conduct in the synagogue–after reading scripture from a standing position, one would sit down to teach and preach. Jesus knew the traditions and rituals and the substance of his hometown synagogue. And he knew, it seems clear, that after abiding in faithfulness in the face of temptation in the desert and before commencing his saving mission and ministry, it would be natural to come home.

In the coming Sundays I will be lifting up the highlighted moments of Jesus' powerful selection of Isaiah 61 as the text for his first, fundamentally formative sermon. For now, allow your heart and mind and soul to dwell on one single phrase from Jesus' powerful oration. Hear those simple words with which he starts: *"The Spirit of the Lord is upon me..."* You can almost miss it if you're not careful. There are far more impressive phrases that follow: *"...good news to the poor...release to the captives...recovering of sight to the blind...liberty [for] those who are oppressed."* If Buck O'Neil were our scripture reader today, he would add his powerful signature style to such powerful phrases. Can't you hear him: "*...good news to the poor*–Yah!...*release to the captives*–Yah!...*recovering of sight to the blind*–Yah!...*liberty [for] those who are oppressed*–Yah!" And such an inflected reading would be completely appropriate, given the powerful dimensions of truth and grace they contain.

But don't neglect the opening phrase Jesus employs: *"The Spirit of the Lord is upon me..."* Seemingly simple, innocent, some might even say commonplace, innocuous, negligible, just an opening phrase. But wait, don't rush past this powerful assertion too quickly. For what Jesus is saying about his life and by direct connection, what he is saying about our lives in this audacious eight-word declaration is this: the finger of God, the mantle of the Holy, or as the text puts it, "The Spirit of the Lord" has touched him!

The Spirit of the Lord has touched Jesus. The Spirit of the Lord will move him to touch others and it will move others to touch him.

The power of touch cannot be over-emphasized in Jesus' life and teachings. Jesus comes eventually and everywhere to touch everybody. And everyone yearns to touch him. Jesus knew intimately the extraordinary power of touching: He touches the same loaf of bread with a tax collector in the tax collector's home and thereafter Zaccheus becomes not only a friend but a philanthropist. He is unafraid to touch lepers, and to heal the blind and lame.

He knows how crucial touch is for others: *"If I only touch [the hem of Jesus'] garment, I will be made well,"* a woman declared (Matt. 9:21). *"People were bringing their little children to him in order that he might touch them..."* (Mk. 10:13).

Jesus knew what we have come to know (either slowly or quickly but usually with some portion of pain): touching is absolutely important in all dimensions of our lives–physically, relationally, spiritually. The sensation of tactile contact–touching–is one of the most necessary elements in human development. Such touching is holy and fine:

- like the touch of a baby's head upon your hand as your cradle her and watch carefully for "the soft spot"...or
- like the touch of an exultant "high five" after two buddies ace their mid-term exams...or
- like the touch of your grandchild's hand as you walk together at World's of Fun–secure, safe, bonded, because of what?–the touch.
- like the touch of someone who loves you by smoothing out your hair, straightening the blanket, as they tenderly say goodnight and tuck you in...or

And it need not be only the touch of human flesh that can be regarded as holy. It can also be...

- the touch of the woodworker's craftsmanship along the edge of a finely fashioned piece of furniture...or
- the touch of a book cover (as a woman once did when I

purchased a brand new, clothbound first edition of Thoreau's *Faith in a Seed*, exclaiming: "Oh, a *real* book!")...or

- the touch of the sun upon your cheek and on the sidewalk, warming you down to your very soul and warming the land (so that this now unwanted winter can finally depart!).

Yes, touch is crucially, irreducibly important. Animals die of marasmus without the stimulation of touch. Senior citizens prolong their lives for impressive additional years beyond the norm when they receive at least five hugs a day. And it is not only the family that prays together that stays together. The family that touches in affection and affirmation together stays together.

The touch of a loving hand, a healing kiss, a warm em brace–all these are precious and holy.

There are other kinds of touch, however. Just two weeks ago, the negative impact of the wrong kind of touching was brought home to me with excruciating poignancy.

A Cutting Question...

A minister colleague and I were sharing some sacred discussion over some sacred tortilla chips and some sacred salsa at Jalapeno's in Brookside. We spoke glowingly of the congregations we are privileged to serve. We shared some tidbits of news about a friend down in Texas, a possibility for a mission outreach project in South Africa, and all the exciting activities going on in preparation for the General Assembly here in Kansas City this coming July. Simple, straightforward "minister-talk," with a healthy sprinkling of references to preaching and worship and God all the rest, like the way we usually talk when we get together. After we finished our meal and paid the tab, we went out to my Jeep to make a quick dash back to work. As I turned on the ignition switch of my Jeep, a woman came up to the window and shoved a piece of paper at us. "Here, read this!" she snarled and then went on her way down the sidewalk, I recognized her from the restaurant. She had been sitting in the booth next to ours. The piece of paper she gave us read as follows: *"How can you, or anyone, worship a God that allows a child to be beaten, raped, and left for dead? God has no compassion for the lowborn."*

Her words were so shocking and unsettling to me that it took me a couple of minutes to recover my composure. I wanted to run after her, square off and say straight-away to her: "I don't, I won't worship that kind of God. Can we talk?" But she was already gone, having slipped away into the anonymous neighborhood and the rest of her day and the rest of her life.

In his book *A River Runs Through It,* Norman McLean says, "I am haunted by waters." I have been, and I am now still haunted by the anonymous woman's question. I am haunted by those words that reflect harsh, hurtful, unholy touching. And, much more importantly, she (and a host of fellow sufferers) have obviously been haunted by touches of brutality, cruelty, and insanity for far too long. Why did she put her question the way she did? Was she the child? Was it her child? Was it a child she knew? Was it a child or was it children that she and you and I read about all too frequently? And what would predispose her heart to be so quick with a condemnation of God about such touching?

The Touch We Need...

Which brings me here, along with you. We've come, when all is said and done, for a certain kind of touching–like unto and indeed very much identical with the Spirit that was upon Jesus in Nazareth and throughout his three years of ministry and beyond.

We come for a touching that can help repair our own personal worlds and a world full of inhabitants who are torn, tattered, sometimes nearly rent asunder by jagging, jabbing, hurtful touching.

Today we come before the throne of grace and within the comforting embrace of this congregation for the touch of God's Holy Spirit upon our lives.

We come seeking such a touch not only for today but for the entire season of Lent and beyond, and if we are disciplined and care-full enough, for forever.

We come remembering Jesus' declaration that the Holy Spirit had touched him with a searing awareness of his mission, and with a clear vision of his mandate.

We come knowing that if we can also be so touched by God's Spirit, we can begin a new healing in the world.

And when God's Spirit rests upon us, we will be able to sing with new meaning, *"He Touched Me!"*

We will be able to touch and allow ourselves to be touched in the enriching, energizing, and enthusing context of the community of faith, otherwise known as the Body of Christ, something God has touched and continues to touch with grace and power to change lives in miraculous ways.

As you come forward to receive the Imposition of Ashes, accept the smudge of an ashy cross upon your forehead as a time-honored ritual *and* also as a touch from on high. Imagine, as well – and perhaps you will even hear deep down in your soul – God speaking a word of encouragement and blessing upon you, saying, in a word, *"touché,* meant not for jousting nor for a wounding, but rather as an annealing touch of healing, hope, humility and holiness that we and the world so desperately need. AMEN and AMEN.

19

The Answer in the Ashes

Text: Daniel 9:1-3

What Do You Do with Your Ashes?

I'd like to ask a question that I've never posed to you before. Since returning to Community's pulpit a few, short three months ago, as you may have noticed, I've been "cuttin' to the chase" a good bit. By that, I mean I believe it really does serve us best to be boldly forthright and do as Frederick Buechner suggests. Here, allow me to steal a line from Shakespeare's magnificent *King Lear*, which Frederick Buechner has borrowed for the title of his latest book: *"The weight of this sad time we must obey,/Speak what we feel, not what we ought to say."*[1] What I want to ask is this: *"What Do You Do With Your Ashes.?"*

It never really occurred to me until this year that this is a wholesale problem in the human community. What *do* you do with your ashes?

This doesn't have to do with fireplaces and dust traps, or coal shoots. This is not about ash trays for cigarette ashes and cigars, nor about the length to which Clarence Darrow would go, so legend has it, to distract a jury from its appointed duty. They say that Darrow used to put a straightened-out paperclip down one of his famous cigars. The paperclip would serve to hold the ash in place, and as a trial would wear on and the jury would wear out, the ever-lengthening ash would attract the attention and invigorate the distraction of the jury. So much so did this strategy work, that, according to legend, the jury began to take bets as to when Darrow's cigar ash would surely fall!

No, I don't mean that kind of ash. Nor am I really inquiring about the various ashes used in ancient cultures and exotic declensions of culture. In olden times, the placing of ashes on oneself, was a symbol of penance, enacted on occasions of ritualistic repentance. Goodness knows that we could use an ample supply of ashes around the world these days. From the Enron hearings in DC to the tribunal for Mr. Milosevic's war crimes to the dilemmas of the Piper School District and its engagement with issues of plagiarism to the consciences of normal every-day Americans doodling with pen and paper as they consider how best to prepare their taxes, we sure could use a whole lot of ashes in the human community.

Of course it has always been a sign and symbol of mourning, as well. Job sits in a pile of ashes and Daniel and Esther and Ezekiel and Isaiah and Jeremiah and Joel and Nehemiah all speak of donning the dry raiment of sackcloth and ashes for an appropriate sign of grieving, both personal and communal.

Of course, it's also always a part the traditions of contrition and confession in the Judeo-Christian heritage. Ashes show forth a penitent heart and a remorseful soul abiding in the believer. Sitting in the ash heap, as in the case of Job, reveals, according to some on-lookers, exemplary pious repentance. Obviously our imposition of ashes today partakes of nearly all of those meanings and significations, but there is also still more.

Daniel Seeks Answers in His Ashes

Daniel had some ashes too. In the book of Daniel, among that extraordinary tome's six stories and four dream-visions, there is a wonderful, yet curious, declaration by Daniel about his yearning attempt to connect with God: *"Then I turned my face to the Lord God, to seek an answer by prayer and supplication with fasting and sackcloth and ashes"* (Dan. 9:3).

The setting is two centuries before Christ's birth and the prophet/envisioner Daniel is confronting the degradation and devastation of Jerusalem and very likely that of Antiochus as well. His way of dealing with the destruction and the dissolution of people and place is to turn to God, to seek an answer in the middle of the ashes. Here is the great and renowned prophet of the lion's den, the one who can read the handwriting on the wall for Nebuchadnezzar, the one who endures a fiery furnace with Shadrack, Meshack and Abednego and escapes without even a tan. Here he is now in an attempt to do something even grander and more mysterious and wondrous still. What Daniel does with his ashes is this: he seeks to discern the answers that are there.

Like Daniel, let us take the ashes of our lives, however we've come to have them, and seek to interpret their meanings. Let me ask you to consider a few questions daringly, honestly, forthrightly: What do you do with the ashes of your disappointments, defeats, disillusionments, despair, and the deaths, real and large, and what Jules Feiffer called our "little deaths"??

What do you do with the ashes of your anger, anxiety, and with what the French call *ennui*, what used to be called (in Latin) *acedia*?

What do you do with the ashes of your hurts, harms, unhealthy habits, and heart-breaking encounters with life?

What do you do with your ashes?

A New Five-Finger Exercise

As we look at the ashes of our lives and seek an interpretation of them, I want to suggest a brand-new *"five-finger exercise"* for us throughout this Lenten season.

You can begin to understand the answer in the ashes – their meaning for your lives – by knowing that you...

(1) *Don't throw our your ashes away. Rather allow them to* FERTILIZE *the garden of your life.* Our losses and failures, our frailties and inadequacies, are great teachers, or at least they can be if we let them. Just consider how much you've learned by the failure experiences in your brief wisp of life on this good earth. I will wager we each have gained far more by those times when we came up short in the grand ledger of existence. If we throw those ashy defeats away, we can't learn from them. If we allow them to fertilize the garden of our life and tend them carefully, we can behold grand and beautiful things blossom around us and in us. I think this is what the 12-step recovery movement is all about: not allowing the ashy experiences of defeat and disillusionment to be silenced or squashed or otherwise lost, but rather using those times to fertilize life into redemption.

- *Consider the fires that have rendered your ashes as* REFINING FIRE, *doing an interior re-fashioning of your entire being.* In the middle of the sabbatical adventure with which you graced Priscilla and me, a startling revelation occurred about something happening inside of me. It really started first inside my pocket. I found something in the frail, tattered "ashen" corners of my pants pockets. I discovered I'd been carrying around in my pocket way too many keys (21 to be exact) for the past 15 years, when all I really need on a daily basis is four. This simple insight was also a huge symbolic shift.

- *Ponder the FREEDOM you have at your disposal in the wake of your losses.* We have all known an ash-heap's worth of tremendous losses this past year. No one in this room needs reminding of the onslaught of ice that stormed through Kansas City just 14 days ago. The ashes of disappointment were everywhere as we waited for heat to return and lights to come on. The ashes of a creeping depression were piled high as we beheld branch after branch and limb after limb of our favorite trees piled higher and higher by the curbs in front of our houses and apartments. But could it be that, in the wake of the brutality suffered by our trees, we have a new freedom to appreciate, really deeply appreciate, the wonderment that trees always are, before, during and after such storms?

  And who will ever forget the traumatizing effects of September 11, when untold tons of ash rained down on hapless victims at the World Trade Center? Who will ever forget those ashen faces of news-reporters, rescue workers, fire fighters, police officers, and countless other New Yorkers, as they contended with the horrific events of that day of sorrows? But who will ever also forget the gallant, courageous actions and attitudes of thousands upon thousands of people in New York City, as they sorted through the ashy rubble of Ground Zero, and we all began the daunting tasks of sorting through our ash-covered debris-strewn lives, seeking answers to life's most perplexing questions on a day which was, as a good friend put it, "the worst day I've ever spent on this planet"? But in that debris and in the ashen black hole of insanity that Ground Zero was, was there not a new found freedom that came? Did you not feel freer to call up those folks who once were "relatives" and now you've reclaimed as "loved ones"? Did we not have more permission, more freedom to weep when we needed to weep, to laugh and embrace when a laughing embrace was in order? And don't you now sense that the time is urgent and we have been freed to love and live with more honesty and immediacy and grace? Please, ponder the freedom you have at your disposal even, and sometimes especially, in the wake of your losses.

- *Count the blessings of God's FAVOR upon your life...in light of what you* don't *have.* This is not merely an exercise in the philosophical notion of *"negative capability."* Rather I'm speaking here of an array of status achievements certain folks have. Some folks get a new job, a new promotion, and there's a new status attained. And those who don't experience those achievements and attainments taste the tang of an ashy *lack* of status on their tongues. To be very frank with you, Valentine's Day, tomorrow's grand tribute to chocolate and the undying art of greeting card "I-love-you's" is not necessarily a thrill to some folks. In a culture which rewards "coupledness," even in our tax structures and in our corporate business cultures, it's not necessarily super to be single on Valentine's Day, is what I'm saying. But please note that I am not advocating for a pity party to be thrown for single folks. No, far from that. I actually want our single friends to count the blessings of God's favor on their lives because of what they *don't* have. You may be without a mate, but you also enjoy the great grace of doing as you please and negotiating reality with a greater ease of thought and adjustment. Yes, single or coupled, you don't have a thick stock portfolio and you don't have that many zeroes congregating on your check each month, and yes, yes, you don't have and you don't have and you don't have...! OK, so that's the case. But did you count your blessings this last year as you watched your buddy's stocks go out the window and down the drain? Did you notice, in your "less-than," "don't-have" status, that your responsibilities over your resources are clear and direct and altogether liberating? Count the blessings of God's FAVOR upon your life...in light of what you don't have.

- *Receive God's FRESH GIFTS in the very midst of the ashes.* There is a gift in the midst of the ashes in our lives, whether they are of the metaphorical type or actual physical type, whether you're feeling those ashes touch your soul, or you are looking at their physical counterpart in the trees outside your living room window.

My friend Don Jen knows all about God's fresh gifts even in the midst of life's ash heaps. Don and Marji's wedding was the first wedding over which I was ever privileged to preside as the officiating minister. We first met at All Peoples Christian Church in south central Los Angeles. We would become roommates and extremely close, and, over the long haul, abidingly good friends. During the course of the sabbatical, Priscilla and I had a chance to enjoy dinner with Don and Marj in San Francisco. Over dinner, he recollected one of my favorite stories of his time in LA. One time, after a trek to the mountains for camping and hiking and the sheer enjoyment that only the Sierra Nevada mountains can bring, Don went back to his house in "the hood" in south central Los Angeles. Where his house had been–where all his clothes were hung neatly in a closet, where his LP's (those beloved old vinyl relics) were racked neatly in an old apple crate, where his sacred stuff, all of his holy possessions, had been, not to mention the house itself–all of it was gone! Burned to the ground! Rendered into a flattened heap of ash! Don, however, didn't weep, didn't cry, but went straightaway to his spiritual family, the All Peoples community of faith. And there he shared his story and there was even a laugh or two. And years later, when Don recounts this story, there is a smile of recognition on his face, and a fond remembrance of when he discovered the answers to some of life's toughest questions in that smoldering ash-strewn square where his house had once stood. And what were the answers in the middle of those ashes? You know what they were–simply this: *Ashes are the purified residue of what's left over, after the burning, after the torrent of fire and annihilation, after all is said and done and gone. Ashes are the essence–either in real, geophysical form or in sacred memory and holy imagination–of what truly lasts.* Ashes are not about detritus but about the real stuff of our real lives. The answer? Though we are not in charge, life can be trusted, because God will give us everything we truly need, in fact al ready has in the presence of a carpenter from Nazareth, who didn't have anything of material worth, but was left hanging on a cross, and yet, who rose up out of the nothingness of death and assured that we'd never, never be alone.

Here we stand, at the commencement of a brand new Lenten journey, perhaps the most important Lenten journey we will ever take in our lives. We are launching into the 40 days between today, Ash Wednesday, and the culmination of Easter, minus the Sundays, of course, which are excluded from the counting because they represent oases of "little Easters" in the wilderness of our Lenten trek.

Here we are, receiving the incessant, urgent, undeniable gift from God in a smudge of ash. There are answers galore in all of these ashes. Receive them and be made whole this Lenten season and always. AMEN and AMEN.

Notes

1 Frederick Buechner, *Speak What We Feel (Not What We Ought to Say): Reflections on Literature and Faith* (New York: Harper San Francisco, 2001).

20

Grace for the Left-Overs

Text: Romans 5:6-8

Welcome by T.S. Eliot

Although I do not hope to turn again
Although I do not hope
Although I do not hope to turn...

Wavering between the profit and the loss
In this brief transit where the dreams cross
The dream crossed twilight between birth and dying
(Bless me father) though I do not wish to wish these things...
This is the time of tension between dying and birth
The place of solitude where three dreams cross
Between blue rocks...

Suffer us not to mock ourselves with falsehood
Teach us to care and not to care
Teach us to sit still
Even among the rocks,
Our peace in His will
And even among these rocks
Sister, mother
And spirit of the river, spirit of the sea,
Suffer me not to be separated

And let my cry come unto Thee."[1]

T.S. Eliot's memorial words for Ash Wednesday serve as the finest introduction I know of for this special holy day on the church calendar. We are all of us hoping to turn and not hoping. We are all of us caught midstride between great new resolutions about faith, about turning over a new leaf in the book of our lives, about turning up the volume of God's love in the soundtrack of our existence, about doing what John the Baptist and Jesus were always preaching about, *metanoia*, turning into a new creature, made new by the power and might of God's gospel of redeeming love.

Today is the beginning of the Lenten journey and, perhaps more so than in any Lenten sojourn in the past, I'm so very glad we're launching into this hoping-but-not-yet-hope-full season. I suppose I need this day and am glad to see it come in the same way that you may need it and are glad to see it come. We are much like T.S. Eliot describes his own time: "wavering between the profit and the loss," immobilized and kept from moving because of a "tension between dying and birth."

"Wavering between the profit and the loss..."

For nearly a year now, and some folks may say the time has been much longer than that, we have been suffering under the direct burden of the economic downturn in the greater Kansas City metropolis. For the first time in a long, long time, our church family has been pained by a worrisome number of layoffs, cutbacks, and stock shrinkages. Perhaps we didn't acknowledge it quite outright, since our membership has always been so loyal and, frankly, we have been blessed mightily by great generosity over the past troubled year. But still we know that hard-times have made life seem like a yo-yo for many people, as they wavered "between the profit and the loss."

In our leadership circles, too, we have been wavering as a congregation "between the profit and the loss," as we've paid heartfelt tribute farewells to three sterling elders in a mere short six months. My, my, how we always miss those princes and princesses in our midst who join the Church triumphant and leave us here wondering if we can ever make it without their singular gifts of joy and insight and wisdom. And how acute the pain is in our missing those who leave us so quickly one after another.

We do make it, somehow. Yes, we do make it, but amidst great tears and sometimes deep fatigue, as we endure a sure sense of Eliot's "wavering" dynamic.

But all of this wavering leads me to understand Eliot's deeper and clearer take on the meaning of Ash Wednesday which goes far beyond profit and loss. Thomas Stearnes Eliot, transplanted St. Louis resident who would become a British-oriented Anglophile, finally understood his life and his poetry as participants in a great drama of life and death and rebirth out of death. Thus his emphasis on the "tension between dying and birth."

"This is the time of tension between dying and birth..."

This really is the time of tension between dying and birth. The horizon of the world is shadowed by specters of war. And everywhere there are deafening rumors of war. Plus, in the middle of the current challenges to stability and security, there are a few fear-mongers who dabbling in the basest sort of superstition and want to play-off of and make money from the fevered apocalyptic nightmares of some folks. (Please note that the date and time of 03-03-03 at 03:03 has passed and the world has not come to an end!)

All of which leads me to think that the metaphor of "Left-Overs" is exactly right for a proper description of how some of us may be experiencing the new millennium and particularly the year 2003. "Left-over" is an apt phrase not only for what we may feel about own lives – caught in the down-spiraling of Sprint's many shake-ups and shake-downs. Left-over – like last year's cold turkey and dressing. Left-over – like a discarded, worn-out coat. Left-over. Passed over. Left-out. Cut-out. Let-down. Down-sized. Down-cast. Down and out, sometimes, even for some folks.

Down but not out, however. "Left-over" is also a decent way of assessing where some folks are spiritually. More than a few of you have expressed to me a wonder-filled sense of exasperated yearning for new life. You want to know what to do with the rest of your working lives. Despite a lay-off, you yearn for new meaning and are deciding that now is as good a time as any to try on your deepest dreams and your fondest hopes to see if they still fit. "Left-over," yes, but not yet dead. Still caught in the tension and leaning toward the birthing end of the scales of life.

Which is where all of us are exactly supposed to be when Lent begins with a smudge of ashy dust on our foreheads – leaning, ever leaning toward birth, and shedding the "dyings" of what doesn't work any more, what is no longer fit for any of our fidelities.

So, on this bleak late-winter Wednesday, let us allow some instruction from two great sources of inspiration, the apostle Paul and, again, T.S. Eliot.

First, some instruction from the man who gave us the original score for "*Cats*," who was himself a very uncool, unhip cat himself.

In his poem "Ash Wednesday," Eliot would hit his stride as a person of hope. Out of the strident and revolutionary thrusts of his early poetry, Eliot grew more positive and less ironic, until 1930 when "Ash Wednesday" was published. Eventually he would receive the high accolade of the Nobel Prize in 1948.

No recipient of that prize has ever moved to the dais in Oslo without having moved into a posture of hopefulness toward life and what is possible for humanity's prospects. So it was for Eliot. And so he would have it be for us.

It is in the latter portions of *"Ash Wednesday"* that I believe we can detect some cues for our Lenten journey toward birthing and hope and redeeming love.

"Suffer us not to mock ourselves with falsehood...

That's what Lent is centrally focused upon, isn't it? Taking a good look in the mirror and seeing ourselves without the mockery of lying to ourselves. And seeing the left-overs of your life for what they are and can be–tremendous blessings for you and others.

Recently, I ran across the clarified story about Leland and Jane Stanford and their establishment of Stanford University in Palo Alto, California. In 1884, when he was barely 16 years old, their son Leland, Jr. died of typhoid fever. They were grief-stricken to the marrow of their very being. But they were equally determined to do something with what was left over of their lives.

Because they were people of some significant means, they fantasized about creating an educational institution. They visited Cornell, MIT, and other prestigious schools in the East. With another Eliot, President Eliot of Harvard, they inquired what it would take, in addition to land and buildings, to establish and endow a university of similar stature and status. With a bit of a sneer, so the legend goes, president Eliot is reported to have replied, "Well, at least $5 million dollars." "Well, Jane," said Mr. Leland Stanford, Sr., "we could manage that, couldn't we?" and a grieving Mrs. Stanford gave her assent.

Thus was born Stanford University. The Stanfords looked at life squarely in the face, without falsehood, and saw themselves for who they were – supremely saddened because of their son's death – and supremely charged to take the left-overs of their life and make something good happen for others. As Mr. Stanford, Sr., out it, "The children of California shall be our children."

"Teach us to care and not to care..."

This puzzling phrase is also instructive for us, especially as we figure out what to do with the left-overs of our existence. Teach us to discern what's deserves our bother, Eliot seems to be saying. Let us live life in such ways that we will care about the best things and become the best kinds of people.

Somehow, I believe Ken Robertson truly knew what to care about and what to let go of. And his family learned the same lesson in discernment. What a blessing it was to me to hear their stories, as we prepared for the celebration of his life. And how hilarious and ultimately holy it was to hear his children and grandchildren tell stories about his card-playing acumen. Ken, as the stories are always told about him, was a great card-player. He won and won and won. But, as one of his grand-daughters put it (in accordance with the assent of the entire family), "You never felt like you lost when he won." To live your life in such way as to deserve such an epitaph, is to learn to care about the best things and focus on being and becoming the best people we are capable of becoming. Another way to put it is this: find out figure out, tease out what truly deserves your bother. And then consider what matters most to pray for, those moments that I call "the necessary poems of our lives, our lives' longest longings," like...

blessings for the babies;
comfort in the hands when held by mothers;
love in the eyes when beheld by fathers;
care in the laps when received by grandmas;

grace in the stories when told by grandpas;
work that does not leave us weeping;
a simple, single day's trek of peace;
the well-formed shape of the fine-tuned song.

I would say that these "*will do. Each one, for sure, deserves our bother.*"[2]

"Teach us to sit still..."

Now comes the hard part. But please remember this is not so much a call to stasis but rather a call to arms, a call to the arms of a loving divine Presence in life who wants us to be blessed. This is what Jesus always wanted form his first followers: to receive the great grace he had to impart to them. From the Sea of Galilee to the Garden of Gethsemane, Jesus always wanted his disciples to let the arms of God's loving holiness to envelope them in such a way that they would never be without warmth again. The apostle Paul put the whole matter like this: "But God shows his love for us in that while we were yet sinners Christ died for us."

While we were yet sinners, God loved us and loves us still.

While we were yet sinners...

while we were yet left-overs...

while we were left out of the job market...

while we were yet bereft of any sense of our truest vocation...

while we were yet lacking in reconciliation with our families...

while we were yet without hopes or prospects of reaching our highest dreams...

while we were yet without any worthiness to speak of...

while we were yet homeless and hopeless and heedless and humorless and honor-less...

while we were yet pavilioned in mansions and yet still

homeless...

While we were yet left-overs...While we are yet sinners... God loves us.

Here we are at the start of a brand new Lenten journey, perhaps the most important Lenten journey we will ever take in our lives. We are launching into the 40 days between today, Ash Wednesday, and the culmination of Easter, minus the Sundays, of course, which are excluded from the counting because they represent oases of "little Easters" in the wilderness of our Lenten trek.

Here we are, receiving the unmistakable mark of our temporariness, our left-over-ness. At the same time, in the same smudge of ashy dust, we are also receiving the undeniable mark of God's generous love.

Let us remember that when God says grace over left-overs, he speaks a clear and distinctive word. It is the holiest prayer we can ever hear: Christ, yes, Christ the Lord. Yes, all you left-overs, hear the word of grace spoken over you this day. AMEN.

Notes

1 T.S. Eliot, "Ash Wednesday," in *The Complete Poems and Plays, 1909-1950* (New York: Harcourt, Brace & World, Inc., 1971), pp. 66-67.

2 Robert Lee Hill, *Hard to Tell: A Congregation of Poems, 1990-2003* (Los Angeles: MOSAIC Impressions, 2003), p. 52.

21

When Grace Gets Real

Texts: Isaiah 58:3-12 and Luke 3:1-6

Lent Begins

Today, on Ash Wednesday, Lent begins. There are a multitude of meanings to be discovered for what this sacred season called Lent really is and what it does for the Christian faith community and the world.

Lent is a time of the lengthening of days and a lengthening of our love for God and for one another. It is a time for enhancing one's life with the rhythms of faith.

Lent is a time for the passing away of the old and the welcoming of the new. It is a time for renewed commitments and fresh, brand new covenants.

Lent is the occasion of journeying with Christ through his wilderness challenges, along the Galilean seashore where he taught and healed, and around his tables of fellowship, knowing that our own wildernesses, our own moments of learning, and our own table talk will be blessed by Christ's presence.

Lent is the blessing of your life with the practice of prayer and the regular opening of your heart to God's Spirit. Lent is the opportunity to acknowledge those dynamics and habits and stuck points which are dying in you (and need to!) and the recognition that resurrection is possible for you and the whole human family because of Christ's merciful grace for us all.

About Lent

The Ashes in today's services mark the beginning of the Lenten season–the 40 days stretching from Ash Wednesday to Easter (minus the Sundays in between). It is 40 actual days prior to Palm Sunday and the beginning of Holy Week and the Passion of Christ leading up to the Triumph of the Resurrection.

The Lenten journey provides Christians perhaps the richest seasonal opportunities for the deepening of our faith. There are more extraordinary occasions for enriching one's life during Lent than during any other one stretch of time on the Church's liturgical calendar. This year at Community I hope and trust you'll participate in as many of the Lenten events for inspiration and education as you possibly can. This year's Lenten program really has been designed to provide something for everybody.

But to quote one of my bold, younger friends when she saw the ashy smudge on my forehead in time's past: "What are the ashes for?" Which is a very good question.

A participation in tradition and heritage

The practice of using or imposing ashes has a long and occasionally confusing and sometimes mysterious heritage. Before the birth of Christ, various cultures, the Hebrews in particular, designated times of fasting, penance, and prayer by placing ashes on their foreheads.[1] We can assume and best understand that the customary use of ashes in the church originated with Judaism.

Sometimes in the 4th century after the birth of Christ,

Christians publicly made their penitence visible by dressing in sackcloth and being sprinkled with ashes as a sign of their feelings of regret for wrong-doing and their new resolve to live uprightly. Regular public displays of penance eventually died out. But somewhere between the end of the 8th century and the middle of the 11th century, it became a regular practice of the Church for the faithful to receive the imposition of ashes at the beginning of Lent before proceeding into a season of repentance in anticipation of Easter's resurrection celebration.

Lent's history is parallel to but also different from the use of ashes by Christians.[2] Lent is a word with Middle English roots–lenten–that means springtime, or the lengthening of days. Originally the days of fasting, penance, and prayer were relegated to a few days just prior to Easter by the early Christians. Then the observance expanded to the entirety of what we now call Holy Week, then further to three weeks, and then to forty days (not counting Sundays) prior to Easter. The figure forty paralleled Jesus' 40 days of fasting and being tempted in the wilderness (see Lk. 4:1-13). This seemed to be a fitting period to prepare with preaching and teaching those who would be baptized on Easter Sunday.

So, this time-honored ritual has had multiple historical angles. Likewise, it has a multiplicity of meanings for each and all of us, personally and collectively

A mark of one's identity

Remember that today's Imposition of Ashes is a way of identifying yourself as a Christian for one day of the entire year. In other words, you have permission today to show your faith to others. The culture grants you that permission, of course in a moment of toleration. "What's that mark on your forehead? Forget to take shower this morning? Oh, yeah it's that ashy day for you isn't it?" Well, go ahead, enjoy the toleration, but use the encounters with others to truly probe your identity. This is the ultimate day to ask "Who am I, really?"

This also the ultimate time to find your particular place in your specific location as the unique manifestation of human protoplasm that is you! Did you notice earlier in the service the specificity and the particularity in the gospel reading from Luke?

In the fifteenth year of the reign of Tiber'i-us Caesar, Pontius Pilate being governor of Judea, and Herod being tetrarch of Galilee, and his brother Philip tetrarch of the region of Iturae'a and Trachoni'tis, and Lysa'ni-as tetrarch of Abile'ne, in the high-priesthood of Annas and Ca'iaphas, the word of God came to John the son of Zechari'ah in the wilderness...

Our lives are lived out, whether we like it or not, as unique, unrepeatable creations of God. The gospel–from the Christmas crèche to the triumph at the tomb on Easter–is always about particular incarnations of grace and love and truth. This Lenten season could be perhaps one of the best of times you've ever been afforded to delve into your special identity as God's special creation. The mark on your foreheads can remind you of your one-of-a-kind identity.

A sign of repentance

Know that the mark of an ashy cross on your forehead is a mark of repentance, and by that I don't mean feeling sorry for yourself all day, and inviting everyone in your office or on your block or in your apartment complex to your pity-party. Rather I mean what *metanoia* truly means. That's the Greek word in the New Testament for repentance, and metanoia means to change into a new creation, the way a caterpillar changes into a air-born, living, breathing, flying stained-glass window. And as traditional stained-glass windows have always done, such a transformed creature can't help but tell a story of grace and light and a magnificent mercy.

A symbol of humility

You can view your ashy cross on your forehead also as a symbol of humility, as you hear us say "Remember that you are dust and unto dust you shall return." Which is what God is recalled as having declared to Adam after the fall (Gen. 3:19). But it is also a description that Abraham has the temerity to use when speaks to God. "I who am but dust and ashes" (Gen. 18:27).

But allow me to draw your attention to a new definition of what it means to be humble: According to one of our own members in the Pastor's Class, one adamant Angel Thurston, *"Being humble means being proud of God!"*

Remembering

And also note perhaps the most important dynamic of Lent and the practice of the imposition of Ashes: remembering.

Remembering who you are. Remembering your faith. Remembering your family and your love for one another. Remembering God. Remembering Christ. Remembering your neighbor as yourself. Remembering not to forget the stranger who just may turn out to be your next best friend. Remembering to pray as often as you brush your teeth. Yes, remembering!

A Starter-Kit for Your Lenten Faith Tune-up

As we proceed into Lent, I want to urge you to make a covenant between you and God with the following priority items of focus:

(1) Worship every Sunday you are in town, barring sickness of course.
(2) Partake of at least half of the Wednesday worship events, at noon or at 6:30 pm.
(3) Pray daily for the increase of Christ's love in the world, for

the healing of our war-torn, strife-wrought world, and for the increase and growth of Community's congregation.

(4) Seek out a relationship that has been in need of reconciliation & forgiveness in your life.

(5) Read at least one of the gospels (Matthew Mark, Luke, or John) completely through, between Ash Wednesday and Easter Sunday.

(6) Learn something new by trying out a new class (Sundays, Mondays and/or Wednesdays) that will stretch your mind.

(7) Retreat from all media (and that includes television, radio, and internet access on your computer) for at least one hour per day, so that you can let your soul rest and be refreshed.

Allow these seven suggestions to suffice as a "starter-kit" for your Lenten "faith tune-up."

Two Words Before We Go

In the lectionary, one of the chosen scriptures for this day – among Presbyterians, Lutherans, Methodists, Catholics, Episcopalians, and a host of other Christians – is today's Isaiah text.

Is not this the fast that I choose:
to loose the bonds of wickedness,
to undo the thongs of the yoke,
to let the oppressed go free,
and to break every yoke?
Is it not to share your bread with the hungry,
and bring the homeless poor Into your house;
when you see the naked, to cover him,
and not to hide yourself from your own flesh?

Which means to be as free and affirming with others as you yearn for God and others to be with you. Which means to do works that promote goodness – can you think of some actions you can take that will do that? – and unfettering anyone and everyone who is being kept from true liberation within the realm of your influence. Which means to promote some radical about-face actions among our fellow citizens, nationally and world-wide.

As a mark of a gentle prophetic witnessing allow me to proffer a currently favorite quote of mine. You can feel free to use this to foster greater personal freedom in someone, however minute or minuscule. I can give you a money-back guarantee that it will brighten someone's day: "Did anyone ever tell you how beautiful you look when you're looking for what's beautiful in someone else?"[3]

Secondly allow me to share a story about Carolyn Forché which illustrates better than anything I can think the title of this Ash Wednesday message: When Grace Gets Real! Carolyn Forché is a poet and essayist and a teacher of English at George Mason University. She's been a political activist in and has a rich, full cultural heritage that reaches from Czechoslovakia to El Salvador to Russia. She's also a homeowner who has known one of the greater tragedies a homeowner can experience. January a year ago, a water main broke, and she and her family suffered extreme damage to their home. "The deluge, as we call it," she remembered, "–we're not supposed to call it a flood because insurance doesn't cover floods–the deluge lightened our burden. It gave me a glimpse of the future,...It allowed me to deal with our personal effects decades before we might have done so, sparing our son, Sean Christophe, the burden of the task. It was devastating and grueling..." 500,000 gallons of icy water coursed into their home over three hours, in the dead of winter, on January 27, 2003. "In the days that followed," she went on, "we were buried under yet another blizzard and left with little that wasn't wet or muddy or gone." She had thought that her study in the basement had escaped harm, since she and her son had packed a barrier of towels and furniture against the door leading downstairs. When she went downstairs later for some "quiet time," as she called it, she discovered several inches of water and her computer sputtering electric hiccups as it hissed and sparked amidst all the damage. She said it was "interesting to see manuscripts swirling in mud. At first I peeled the pages apart and separated them with paper towels. Then I realized that this was futile, that I had to accept the destruction. This was the rule that would govern my life: I might not be able to choose what happens to me. I might not be able to guide my future, but I could control my response to what happens, and if I could respond beautifully, with love and lightness of heart and a willingness to give up whatever I had to give up, that was what was going to be important for my future year – not the water and the mud."[4]

Carolyn Forché knows what it means when grace gets real! And there's no one and no thing that can take that away from her. May it be so with you and me, as we seek "to respond beautifully, with love and lightness of heart" to whatever happens to us and live with a willingness to give up whatever we have to give up, so that we can embrace whatever God wants to give us, today and always. Ash Wednesday blessings! AMEN.

Notes

1 See Esther 4:1-3, 2 Samuel 13:19, Job 42:6, and Jeremiah 6:26)

2 For the history of Lent and the Christian use of ashes see *The HarperCollins Encyclopedia of Catholicism* (San Francisco: HarpersSanFrancisco, 1995), Thomas O'Brien, editor.

3 Author Unknown (Thanks to Jennie Malewski for this quote)

4 *"A Conversation with Carolyn Forché," IMAGE: A Journal of The Arts and Religion,* Summer 2003, Number 39, pp. 53-69.

22

Worth the Waiting

Text: Isaiah 40:28-31

A Time of Paradoxes

I'm not exactly sure when my fascination–should I say enrapturing?–with Ash Wednesday and the rest of the Lenten season became such a consistent passion for me. I suppose it dates to the time when I commenced my journey in faith with you here in Kansas City. Even in Divinity School back in Nashville, Ash Wednesday and all the rest of the days that mark the procession to Easter's grand and glorious day of resurrection didn't hold much fascination for me. Oh, I knew plenty of Catholics and Episcopalians back then, and more than just a few Lutherans and a couple of Orthodox folks as well. But despite all the smudgy foreheads I beheld back then, it was really my turn toward the heart of the heart of the country that set my mind, heart, and soul always favorably inclined toward the meanings and messages that Lent, in general, possess for all earnest pilgrims through its landscape, and for this day in particular.

A host of reasons present themselves for nomination as "the reason" for the bold, strong attraction to this day, not only in connection to me but with countless other Christians. The strongest contender, I think, is the paradoxical character of this day and what Lent is all about. The paradoxes are paramount!

- The Lenten season begins when seemingly everything else is over.
- We like the fixed predictability of Christmas, the other high and holy day on the Christian calendar, but Lent baffles us most years, with its movable feast character, tied, as it is, to the phases of the moon. (And we're really baffled in a year like this one, when Lent comes so early – and with so much snow! Aren't the crocuses supposed to be about ready to bloom, isn't that when Lent's springtime glory is supposed to happen?)
- Lent announces the warmth of God's presence but it does so when temperatures approach and drop below freezing.
- In the midst of learning about the glorious gift of faith that ought to send us cart-wheeling we hear the call to penance.
- The Lenten saga is perhaps more glorious and meaningful than the Christmas drama. In fact, some might say that without the Lenten journey, complete with the pathos and tragedy and triumph of Holy Week, the Christmas story is just a nice, un-validated romance. (In other words, "No glory with the gory!")
- The ashy smudge on our forehead seems to soil us and yet, because of its burning, its very probably the purest thing with which we ever adorn our faces.

The paradoxes are in part what fascinate me – and I would add you, too – at this time of year.

Waiting

Among all the problematic and pulse-raising paradoxes is

the amount of *waiting* that goes on in this season. For God's sake, Christmas is, at most, four weeks long, But no! Lent is seven weeks of wilting, lethargy-inducing waiting. Forty days–if you don't count the Sundays (known as "Little Easters"). Wait, wait, wait.

We know the way the plot-line of the story goes, we know who wins in the end, or at least, after hearing it all of our lives, we have a pretty good bead on the plot line. But, what do we do? Do we pronounce the victory? Do we dance in the streets when Jesus heads for the wilderness? Do we hoot-and-holler with the Master, winking at death and the demonic temptations he experiences in the desert with the Malevolent One? No, we parallel the Master's experience in the close of his external and internal battles with "desert" conditions. And like him, we wait. And wait. And wait some more. It's almost un-American how we wait.

Waiting doesn't enjoy a very good reputation

Just listen to the litany of condemnations about "waiting."

- *"How much of human life is lost in waiting."*–Ralph Waldo Emerson.

Sometimes waiting is the object of a comic ridicule, like when comedian Steve Wright opines:

- *"I took a course in speed waiting. Now I can wait an hour in only ten minutes."*
- *"Are you really listening...or are you just waiting for your turn to talk?"*–Robert Montgomery.
- *"Being on the tightrope is living; everything else is waiting."* –Karl Wallenda.

We wait, and wait, and then wait some more. And none of it seems to profit any of us much and sometimes not even one smidgeon of life.

Oh, how we wait! At...

- grocery lines at Brookside Market and at the restroom lines at Arrowhead Stadium and at Kauffman Stadium.

  Oh, how we wait! At...
- bookstores and on-line for the next Harry Potter book to come out, and at the telephone, when that juicy job is supposed to be presented for our approval.

  Oh, how we wait! At...
- doctors' offices, and dentists' offices and at the post office. When was the last time you went to see your internist and they said, *"We've been waiting for you! So come in and let's tend to your needs right away!"*

  Oh, how we wait!...
- for the lottery to hit big-time, and
  for the ships to come and
  for the cows to come home, and
  for our chicken s to hatch.

And all the while we know that some of us are city slickers who have no idea what agrarian level-headedness is all about.

And yet, and yet, Lent is simply and ever a time for waiting:

- Waiting for the king of glory to make his ways known upon the earth.
- Waiting for the tragedy of the betrayal of Jesus to be trumped by the triumph of the resurrection of Christ.
- Waiting for Peter (in his abandonment) and for Thomas (with his inquisitive doubting) and for James and John (with their brazen boldness) to play out their parts in Jesus' drama.
- And then waiting by that empty tomb with the women, to see something for the first time, like no one else ever sees—the abandoned cloth, the absence of the body, and then to hear that voice, mistaking it as they did, as any of us

would, for the gardener.

The difference about this sort of waiting is its holiness. This kind of waiting is what faith is all about.

Not instant belief, but waiting.

Not absolute certainty in a blinding flash, but waiting for new light.

Not liberation on a wholesale basis. But waiting and waiting and still more waiting for freedom to become real, one person at a time, one soul at a time, one struggling faith-expression at a time.

Remembering Isaiah

Isaiah gives us a key this year for understanding how holy all of our waiting will be. Did you hear the good news in what the prophet proclaimed?

(1) It's not our own sense of "Carpe Diem" that will pull us through. It's not our own indefatigableness that works. We all should know that by now. Isaiah reminds us that "*The LORD is the everlasting God, the Creator of the ends of the earth. He does not faint or grow weary, his understanding is unsearchable.*"

(2) Isaiah reminds us that when we grow weary in our waiting and when the lactic acid of faint-heartedness has built up in our souls, then we will receive power and strength. When we are weak, just as the apostle Paul will say some 800 years after Isaiah, then we will be made strong.

(3) And those who wait for the Lord will renew their strength. And no matter their, walking or running, we will be given fortitude to finish our race.

Learning How to Wait

Well, I see that some of you aren't buying this, at least not just yet. Allow me to make some suggestions for how we wait.

(A) *Wait with the anticipation that a love lived out daily will bear much fruition in your life.* Just this past Monday I received a very special word of grace from Geneve Selsor, as she bequeathed me her wisdom: "Use your words with charity and then expect that they will be accepted." What a wise, wise word for waiting during Lent.

(B) *Wait for a surprising confirmation to come your way*–about your love life, about your work situation, about your family, about your own faith commitment, about the importance or frivolity of your hobbies.

(C) *Wait for the Lord, either verbally out loud (in the privacy of your own home) or in the secret nooks and crannies where no one seems to ever look.* And behold if the Lord doesn't show up every time.

(D) *And wait for the Lord in the midst of this wintry time* and this season of our nation being at war and the red-state/-blue-state enmity and all of your dieting for the umpteenth time and your not having-enough-time-for-everything-and-everybody-in-your-life and the coldness of so many harsh financial realities and the chilly wind of international tension and the daily death tolls and the ceaseless waterfall of too-much-information, too-much-information, too-much-information and never-enough-wisdom.

And if we will at least begin to learn how to wait like this –upon the Lord, upon what God will do in our lives, upon the entrance of the presence of the Divine into every question and every and quandary, into every conversation and commiseration, into and exploration and exasperating dead-end–if we will learn how to wait thusly, we shall learn what Albert Camus knew: *"In the depth of winter, I finally learned that within me there lay an invincible summer."*

And the winter of any discontent shall be transformed into the spring-time of a satisfying discovery–that God's "Eastering" power to resurrect knows no bounds! And then our springtimes will be transformed into a Pentecostal summer of true invincibility, and we shall claim and be claimed by a strength we never knew we had and a holy justice that we only had thought was a fairy tale and an enduring mercy that we never dreamed was possible.

But first, we wait.

Allow the smudge of an ashy cross upon your forehead be a positive sign for you to wait, wait, wait, upon the Lord to renew you and refresh you and forgive you and fortify you in faith this year's Lenten journey. And may the waiting keep you walking and running in such fashion until your soar like an eagle. May the imposition of ashes remind you that God has been waiting all along for the opportunity to bless you with grace. Amen.

23

Who Is He, Really?

Text: John 14:1-12

Ash Wednesday: A Time for Finding Out Who We Are

Ash Wednesday is a prime time for finding out who we are. You might even say it's the premier occasion for understanding our identity as Christians, or at least beginning to understand anew our identity as Christians, in a very complex, confusing, and occasionally deceptive world. We're searching all the time–aren't we?–at the self-help shelves at bookstores, at class reunions, in mid-career shifts to new jobs, at the gym, in the sanctuary of hearts when we pray–and now comes a moment when the searching has a new and powerful possibility of being fulfilled. It's as if we showed up at the door of the chapel, and said: *"I heard that I can find out who I am in this church. Is this the right place?"* Or, just like we sang to commence this worship service, *"Here I am, Lord! Now would you mind telling me what I'm doing here?!"*

Finding Out Who Jesus Is

The challenge this Lenten season is to find out who we are

by discovering and re-discovering some very interesting insights and revelations about who Jesus is for each of us individually, for all of us together, and for the world.

If you're looking for insights and revelations about who you are and who Jesus is, the gospel of John is an excellent resource for holy awareness and practical knowledge. John's gospel is a unique repository for several of the unveilings of Jesus' true character and purpose. There may be no better method for the discovery of who Jesus is than taking John's gospel and perusing the multitude of Jesus' *"I am..."* sayings in it.

Starting today and for the next few weeks we're going to do just that. We're going to journey through seven of the great *"I am..."* sayings by Jesus in John's gospel. Today we start our trek by considering one of the most dramatic and momentous of the *"I am..."* sayings.

The 14th chapter of John is one of the most beloved and cherished passages of the New Testament. It is full of gravitas but it also rises like a helium-filled balloon on a hot day with its effusive confidence in God's saving love.

At the beginning of the chapter Jesus is saying "good-bye" to his disciples. He has been breaking bread with them. He has washed their feet. Then he uses the occasion of their gathering to offer them (and us) a summary of his core identity. And his hope, the story shows, is that they might discover their truest, highest destiny, their best selves.

John's account of Jesus' "farewell" discourse includes the now famous exchange between Thomas and Jesus. Thomas expresses his doubts – naturally and succinctly – and thus prompts Jesus' clearest declaration of who he is. Thomas' question is about location, where Jesus is going as he leaves them. But Jesus' answer has more to do with existential vocation than it does with temporal location. He says, *"I am the way, the truth and the life."*

The Way

In effect, Jesus is saying *"You don't need an address, a map, a set of coordinates for the place where I am going. Just be and abide with me. The place is not as important as the person you're with in that or any other place."*

I've sometimes described stewardship from a perspective different from our normal takes on the "S" word. Rather than talk about money, we've begun to understand increasingly that Jesus offered us an invitation to a new way of being with God and with one another. Here's the definition: *"Jesus gives us a way of life—resplendent with possibilities for joy, mercy, justice, grace, redemption, forgiveness, reconciliation, and wholeness—and then he bids us, he calls us to give that way of life to others."* This is what it means to say that Jesus is "the way."

I treasure also the way that Fred Craddock prays each morning: *"Lord, I thank you for giving me a way of life that's more important than any way I feel about it on a given day."* Jesus says and we find ever more believable each and every day that his way of life is the best way of life we could ever imagine. (Not so coincidentally, *"The Way"* is one of the first names for the communities that called themselves Christian.) This way, after all, is a way that we'd never give up, a *"road"* as some translations (like Eugene Peterson's) prefer, a route to that which is really real and fully vibrant.

The Truth

Jesus' response to Thomas's doubting also has to do with truth. Now, Jesus is totally unlike Colonel Jessup in *"A Few Good Men."* You'll recall how Jessup took the witness stand and was asked to tell the truth. *"You want the truth?"* Jessup declaims with a sneer. *"You can't handle truth!"* But Jesus says, *"You want the truth? I* am *the truth."* Now please note that Jesus doesn't declare a propositional truth or a doctrinal position of any sort. He doesn't recite a complicated creed about himself, or the manner in which the cosmos has been constructed or humanity's status before God. He simply says, *"I am...the truth."* This is not a debate about a theological proposition but rather an invitation to know a person and the deep truths that arise in a relationship with him.

If we're honest, as Thomas was eventually honest, Jesus is challenging the lies by which we human beings confuse and deceive and warp our lives. Lies like:

"Wealth is a sign of God's blessing."

"There really is no justice in the world."

"The mercy of God is available only in a limited supply."

"God helps those who help themselves."

"Might makes right."

"Some folks are really more precious to God than others."

"Your value is equal to what you possess." (The shorter version of this one is *"You are what you own."*)

All lies, Jesus says. They are, as John Fowles (famed author of *The French Lieutenant's Woman* and a fine poet who sadly died too soon last year) put it, "desert-making heresies." Remembering a time when he and his compeers were not at their best, Fowles describes *"that desert-making heresy/That happiness is having what one lacks."*[1] Jesus says in John's gospel account *"If you know me and the truth that I am, you'll be empowered to live a life in which you never lack for anything that truly matters."*

This Lenten season, allow me to urge you to give up something new. Instead of chocolate or desserts – and thus transforming Lent into some sort of diet plan (some strange version, like the *"Sonoma Lenten Diet,"* or the *"South Beach Lenten Diet"*) – give up one or two of the little lies by which we sometimes live our lies. Perhaps they'll be among the ones I've already cited or maybe you have some special secret ones. Whatever lie you choose, give it up for Lent. And take on the truth of Jesus in your daily walk. You may not lose any weight but ultimately your soul will be a lot healthier.

The Life

And Jesus also says he is "the life."

Not play acting, but life.

Not chicanery and faking it, but authentic life.

No rehearsal, but rather the actual, authentic performance of living.

And not just any life, but the ultimate abundant life that God wants everyone to have.

The season of Lent and the spiritual disciplines associated with it are too often associated with privation, denial, and what sometimes amounts to self-denigration. Jesus' call to check your egos at the door of his way of life is not a condemnation of human existence. It's really about lengthening your life, lengthening your faith, lengthening your relationship with God and with others. That's one of the root origins for the word *"Lent"* itself, *"the lengthening"* of days in the springtime. To Thomas and to us, Jesus is saying, *"Come, lengthen your life and your love, stretch your understanding and your curiosity, widen your grasp of God and the gifts God wants to give you today, right now, in and through me."*

Who Is He, Really? The Sermon On Your Forehead

The question that sits atop this sermon as its title, which is the focusing question for our whole Lenten series of Sunday morning sermons, is one of those persistently important, crucial questions of the ages: *"Who Is He, Really?"*

Who is this Jesus?...for the student and the teacher, for the boss and the employee, for the husband and the wife, for the brother and the sister, for the innocent newbie Christian and the barnacled veteran, for the powerful and the powerless, for the insiders and the outsiders, for the good, the bad and the ugly, for you and for me.

As you receive the smudge of ashes rendered from last year's palm crosses and Palm Sunday fronds, co-mingled with all the years before for nearly a generation, let the horizontal line represent Jesus as the Way that can liberate you out of every situation where you feel or think or believe you are caught or hindered, the Way of Life that is resplendent with possibilities for grace for you.

As you receive the vertical line of ash, let it represent the Truth which Jesus is, above all the lies by which we too often let our lives be governed. The Truth that God is love. The Truth that there is enough divine mercy for everyone. The Truth that God wills us to enjoy faith and church and families and work to the deepest extent imaginable.

And then let the resulting cross on your forehead stand for The Life that Christ gives to you and me, freely and abundantly. The Life that is above and beyond any kind of life that we have ever imagined living, a resurrected life, each and every day.

And as you walk from this place, as you greet others along the way, as you deepen you're faith, the sign on your forehead will become a sermon itself. Leaning ever closer toward Easter's great Good News, your life will be quite a sermon indeed. Let it be so. Let it be so. AMEN.

Notes

1 John Fowles, ***Poems*** (New York: Ecco, 1973)

Christmas Proclamations

24

Candles of Grace

Texts: Isaiah 9:2, 6-7; Luke 2:1-14; John 1:1-14

Good evening! And, once more, Merry Christmas! Tonight, all around the world Christians are gathering like we are here–

- in a strong solidarity
- in simple sympathy
- in soaring celebration.

And all of what we do takes place around a simple powerful, gathering symbol. Tonight is a night for lights!

We come to this night of lights for a hundred thousand reasons.

- Some of us have been coming to this appointed time on the calendar, as long as we can remember. We can't have Christmas without the events of Christmas Eve.
- Some of us are here because of a sense of family responsibility, because of connections with our extended families, especially because of our extended families. We say, quietly in the sanctuary of our hearts, this is what families do, no matter what shape they are, in all of their uniqueness.
- Some of us are here on this night of lights because we are fed-up with the commercialization of the season, and we're here to re-discover the real "reason for the season."

- Many, if not most of us, are here to bask in the glow of the story, the story of all stories, re-told, re-lived, of how God's love for this earth became real beyond dispute in the form of a baby.
- Some of are here with families and friends that are precious to us beyond description, and with many we don't know and may never see again, because we delight in the unity, exhilaration, and soul-stretching joy that fills us to the brim as we remember how God shines glory on the world, again and again, in the winter of its discontent.

AND, we come to this place, this time, with these people, because this is a night of lights.

The Story of the Light

What else could we do, knowing that the story of the light stretches back forever. From creation's dawning, to this very cold December 24, 2004, in the middle of Kansas City, Missouri, the story of God's light of love and grace beams its message down through the millennia.

Isaiah foretold it: *"The people who walked in darkness have seen a great light."* With eager expectation and more than a few down-heartening setbacks, the people of Israel knew that their deliverance would come from the light-bearer, the one who would be *"Wonderful Counselor, Might God, Everlasting Father, Prince of Peace."*

The gospel writer Luke, in his version of the Christmas birthing, also paints a word-picture of the light.

With your sanctified imaginations, picture what Luke calls the glory of the Lord shining down and around those hapless shepherds. Imagine, for a moment that brilliant shining was a combination of all the light displays you know of in the greater Kansas City metropolis. Take...

- the cascading, rainbow waterfall of electric brilliance that shimmers down the face of the downtown Marriott Hotel,

and add to that...

- the forest of blazing illumination at Crown Center,

and add to that...

- the Plaza lights, with its 14 square blocks covered by 80 miles of lights, consisting of 288,000 bulbs,

and add to that

- every Christian congregation observing Advent for the past four weeks, lighting the flames of hope, peace, joy, and love, and then, tonight, the Christ candle in the center of untold incendiary rings of illumination,

and add to that

- the millions of luminarias that surround thousands of churches around the world, especially in Mexico, the origin of that special lighting heritage,

and add to that

- our own "Steeple of Light" and all of its 1.2 billion candle-power of illumination.

Gather all of those beautiful and breath-taking moments of light, and imagine that that would be one-one-hundredth of one-tenth of a percent of the glory that nearly blinded and stupefied the wonder-struck shepherds.

New Meanings This Year

This Story of the light has come into this season's experiences with new meaning this year.

(1) Someone–I really can't figure out who–"spammed" my e-mail in-box with a *"Bless This Day"* message, regarding a "Rapping Baby J." At first I thought it was a weird and crass example of what my friend Chuck calls the "Californianizing" of our culture. But I listened and watched the glowing, haloed figures on my computer screen with fascination and received another message about God's gift of light at Christmas.

The *"Rapping Baby J"*[1] is unique and, to some ears and eyes, I would suspect, hilarious. The chorus from the stylized crèche scene, with a sun-glassed Joseph and hip-looking Mary, sings:

Christ, Christ, Baby,
Christ, Christ, Baby.

Then the little baby Jesus bounds out of the crib and begins singing,

It's Christmas Day–Pray, pray
I'm Baby J
It's my birthday today!
Come and Pray–Pray, pray
I'm Baby J
It's my birthday today!

Then the three Wise Men chime in:

Go Jesus, It's your birthday!
Go Jesus, It's your birthday!

Then the animals surrounding the manger–a donkey, a horse, and two sheep–join in the glad declaration:

You down with G - O - D?
Yeah, yeah! JC!
You down with G - O - D?
Yeah, yeah! JC!
Who's down with G - O - D?
Every last homie!

This is easily the height of cultural kitsch–the setting of the sacred story of Jesus' birth in the sing-songy rhythms of a rap song. And yet...the message of that lighted e-mail message, as kitschy and Californianizing as it may be, somehow reflects the light of imagination and creativity that yearns to shine forth a new declaration, a new way of telling the old-old story.

(2) Then there's the way the Story of the Light comes to us in more profound ways, say any of us is in the midst of pain during this season.

Say, you're battling a cold, and the cold develops into something the biologists haven't even discovered yet, a mutation of pandemic plague proportions. And the cold lodges somewhere deep in your lungs, until you begin to sound like Darth Vadar, on your worst day, or Darth Vadar's voice, James Earl Jones announcing CNN News, on your best days.

Then add to that circumstance, a toothache, and then a

session with the dentist, straight out of the movie Marathon Man, who brings out those three-feet-long needles. Two cavities filled later, with enough novocain to deaden half of the left side of your body.

Now put the Darth Vadar cold together with the post-dental pain. The coughing stimulated by the cold seers a pain straight to your jaw. Raising up in pain because of the jolt to the jaw, your breathing ceases stimulating another cough, and then...you get the picture. Put both of those experiences together simultaneously, and there comes bolt of lightning pain the likes of which you've never experienced in your coughing, cavity-filled life.

But the message of the Story of Light is declared even then. The message? In moments like those, and really in all moments, we are absolutely dependent on others–like caring co-workers who sympathize and support, like Dr. Pat, who is no dentist from any movie, but an actual angel of mercy, whose ways with a drill are really divine and saved the day; like receptionist Terry whose soothing reassurance paves the way for final relief.

And in the midst of that pain you discover the One whose name we always cry out when we are convulsed in paroxysms of pain: "O God! O God!" And that is another meaning of the Story of Light. Exactly. In all of life, even in the midst of pain, perhaps especially in the midst of pain, we are dependent on Someone outside ourselves Who helps us and heals us and holds us ever close to a comforting, eternal heart of grace.

Then you realize the ever-more pained places and people around the world, and an "Oh God!" cries out from them with even greater power. The lightning bolt of devastation, delirium, and destruction goes with blinding speed through the famine-weary Sudan, and the and hate-weary Middle East, and war-torn Iraq and Afghanistan, and the illumination is everywhere, far more unimaginably painful than any tooth or cough could ever be. But, still we face inglorious light of a cry and a truth that are utterly unavoidable: "Oh God! Oh God!"

(3) But tonight the arc of the Story of Light reaches its zenith in a glow more treasurable more than any other light. Tonight we come to light candles, and let us call them, tonight and forever, candles of grace.

This is where the Story of Light becomes really real. This is when we are invited, encouraged, perhaps even compelled to know the story of God's light of grace and love with a deeper understanding than we ever have before. This is my hope, this my dream, this is my prayer for each and every one of you:

Receive your candle this evening as a special message of love for you. Simply receive it, take it in your hands and ponder the sheer, stupendous simplicity of what God is doing in our midst. Think to yourself: "This candle represents the love of God has for the world, including me." Know that you are blessed life and love making you far more than merely a blob of protoplasm in an uncaring expanse of a meaningful void. Rather, as John's gospel has it, you are aglow with God's "power to become not children of God, who [are] born not of blood or of the will of the flesh or of the will of man, but of God."

Then, when you light your candle–as you say silently to yourself what we always silently say, "This is the night we light candles!"–when you light your candle, light it as a candle of grace. Light your candle to grace the world with a simply, unconquerable beauty and supreme truth: that all of the squelching darkness of the world has not, does not, or as Eugene Peterson translates it, "cannot" overcome God's light.

Then would you do one more thing? This is what I sometimes might call "the homework" portion of the message, but's really intended now as a gift for you and yours. When you leave, take your candle with you as a small reminder of the grace with which you can illumine some one's life. Like...

A loved one whom you love and care for and who will cherish your saying, "I love you." Say it to them. You can't say it often enough. Be someone's own "Secret Santa," and give them the gift that truly keeps on giving: the memory of love expressed with endearment and care.

And then remember that the grace of night need not be kept to just one night, indeed cannot be kept to one night. The candles of grace we light on Christmas Eve are sentinel reminders of the lighting of the world that awaits enkindling, wherever we go, wherever we live, whatever we're doing, with whomever we meet. "This is the night we light candles!" Yes! And "This is the life in which I can light a candle each and every day wherever I am, for however long I live." And Yes, to that, too! Yes Indeed!

"This is the night we light candles!" Think it, say it, ponder that phrase with new eyes this night. "This is the night we light candles!" Aglow in that repeated truth, may you all know how much God loves you. May we express such wondrous love to each other. And may you also know this: I love you, dear people of God! Thanks be to God that this is the night we light candles. Merry Christmas and Amen!

Notes

1 http://l.blesstheday.com/redir.cfm/11590/83717/11368/8594346

25

The Holly of Hope on Christmas

Texts: Matthew 1:18-25 and Luke 2:1-20

On Christmas Day, we are still speaking of trees. During Advent's approach to the Christmas crèche we've been talking about *"The Jesse Tree," "The Forest of Peace," "The Family Christmas Tree,"* and, last night on Christmas Eve, *"Three Trees of Love."* Before we proceed through the twelve days of Christmas, we have to give a nod to the Holly, *Ilex aquifoilum.*

The Holly tree's very name connotes sacredness. Holly, holy. For as long as people have been paying attention to trees, the Holly has been associated with mystery and holy power, both within Christian tradition and outside of it.

In Scandinavian countries, the Holly has been believed to have the capacity to ward off evil. For instance, because of its crooked branches, the Holy has been associated with an ability to protect people from lightening strikes. Interestingly enough, the Holly tree does conduct lightening into the ground better than most trees, with the least injury to the tree."[1]

In Celtic culture, the Holly was believed to be the sentinel of winter, and its powers were translated eventually into the mythology of the "Holly King." Eventually, the "Holly King" found its way into the legends of King Arthur and the Green Knight who would do battle with Sir Gawain at a Yuletide feast, bearing a weapon of a "solitary branch of holly."

In Christian tradition there is an association between the Holly and protection. Holly trees were believed to have been at one time deciduous trees–that is seasonally shedding their leaves–until Herod's minions set out on the mission of slaying all the young born of Bethlehem, including baby Jesus. At Mary's request, so the story goes, the Holly tree grew its leaves back so it could hide the Christ within its branches.

Let the Holly tree be a symbol for us this morning of the hope that is given to the world because of Jesus' birth. Because Jesus was protected from Herod–with or without the assistance of the Holly tree–he would grow up and live out his mission of love, grace, mercy and strong compassion. And thus we can have hope that these gifts will be ours as well–to receive and to share with a world much in need.

Let us pause to consider the words of the carol *What Child Is This*, set to the tune of *"Greensleeves."*

What Child is this who, laid to rest
On Mary's lap is sleeping?
Whom angels greet with anthems sweet,
While shepherds watch are keeping?
This, this is Christ the King,
Whom shepherds guard and angels sing;
Haste, haste, to bring Him laud,
The Babe, the Son of Mary.
So bring Him incense, gold and myrrh,
Come peasant, king to own Him;
The King of kings salvation brings,
Let loving hearts enthrone Him.
Raise, raise a song on high,
The virgin sings her lullaby.

Joy, joy for Christ is born,
The Babe, the Son of Mary.

Another Christian legend has it that the Holly tree was present not only at Jesus' birth but also at the end of his human journey when he died upon the cross. The berries of the Holly tree, so the legend has it, were once white, until they were touched by the blood of Jesus when a Holly wreath served as Jesus' crown. None of which is actually, factually verifiable, so far as science has ever been able to determine, but the Holly tree–once again as a symbol of hope–can represent the power of God to transform the world–if not white berries into red, then at least a death into a resurrection, aimlessness into purpose, despair into joy, loneliness into belonging isolation into community.

So, this morning, let the Holly tree remind us that there is hope for us, even when we know neither our own way nor the ways of God in the world. Even though we didn't know who he was, the Christ child would prove eventually that there is always cause for hope. And this is so, even when we can hardly understand why or what we are singing. Let us hear then, with new ears this Christmas morning, *"Sweet Little Jesus Boy."*

Sweet little Jesus Boy,
they made you be born in a manger.
Sweet little Holy Child,
didn't know who You were.
Didn't know you come to save us, Lord;
to take our sins away.
Our eyes was blind, we couldn't see,
we didn't know who You were.
Long time ago, you were born.
Born in a manger low,
Sweet little Jesus Boy.
The world treats You mean, Lord;
treats me mean, too.
But that's how things is down here,
we didn't know 'twas You.

You have showed us how,
we are trying.
Master, You have showed us how,
even when you were dying.
Just seems like we can't do right,
look how we treated You.
But please, sir, forgive us Lord,
we didn't know 'twas You.
Sweet little Jesus Boy,
born long time ago.
Sweet little Holy Child,
and we didn't know who You were.

At the end of Christmas Day rituals experienced by the boy narrator in Dylan Thomas' *"A Child's Christmas in Wales,"* there is the following reflection:

"...and then I went to bed. Looking through my bedroom window, out onto the moonlight and the unending smoke-colored snow, I could see the lights in the windows of all the other houses on our hill and hear the music rising from them up the long, steadily falling night. I turned the light [gas] down, I got into bed. I said some words to the close and holy darkness, and then I slept."[2]

Tonight, Christmas night, as you go to bed, say a prayer of wonder and awe in the presence of the *Sweet Little Jesus Boy*, the One about whom we sing *What Child Is This*, who did in fact come–in love, in generosity and grace and, of course, in loving hope for you and for all the world. Be sure to offer your thanks for his coming. And then after greeting the close and holy darkness with your thanks, sleep with exceeding hope and comforting peace. And offer a "Merry Christmas" to the world once more!

Notes

1 www.paghat.com
2 http://www.bfsmedia.com/MAS/Dylan/Christmas.html

26

Unto You

Text: Luke 2:11

Two little words. "Unto you..." These are the real, foundational presents of this holiest of seasons. These are the ultimate gifts from a gracious God.

"Unto you." Listen. Did you hear the implications? Did you hear the ramifications of that glorious birth announcement from the cosmic maternity ward watchers, those band of angels in the heavenly host?

"Unto you." Like other epigrammatic statements in the Bible, this one packs a wallop of a meaning. Though they are meek and mild (like the Christ Child in the Bethlehem crib) they have significance far outstripping their apparent reach.

"Unto you." It is not unlike the situation when someone sings "Happy Birthday!" to you. The words are just for you. For no one else. Just for you. They are sung, of course, millions of times, in a million different keys, and with a million different inflections and intonations. But when it is your birthday, and everyone is singing for you, that's mystical, nearly magical. Powerfully few words, which contain a powerful message of love and affection.

Last Sunday, Richard, along with a few other hundred folks, gave me a good and holy gift. At the conclusion of the 10:30 worship service in the sanctuary, after I had put in last minute highlight "plugs" for the various and sundry services and activities going on around here this week, our Associate Minister, Rev. Richard Woodard, spoke an aside to me, something to the effect that he had an announcement to make. Then he went to embarrass me by sharing with the congregation that that particular day was, in fact, my birthday. Then, naturally enough, the congregation spontaneously sallied forth with a lusty version of "Happy Birthday." Along with the precious gifts which came from my family, most especially from Priscilla, the singing of that song on that bright Sunday morning was nearly the best birthday present I received this year.

Why? Because those words were particularized. Like "...unto..." Just one person. And, I think you'd agree, you have felt something quite similar, when you have heard the embarrassingly personal strains of that very personal meeting with someone's personal affection and affirmation.

Now, consider. Think on the very personal address which the angelic horde gave to the awe-struck shepherds. "Unto you..." Remember to whom these first words came. Shepherds. Low rung on the social totem pole. Sluggards, laggards, occasionally called low-lifes. Not really the sort of folks who have their pictures emblazoned across the covers of *The Independent*, or *Newsweek*, or *Time* magazines. These were the rough and tumble hombres of their day, similar to the real flesh-and-bone cowboys of times gone by in the American west. With mud on their footwear, aching in their muscles, squint lines around the corners of their eyes from all those days in the hot sun, and with a weariness in the souls, these shepherds were the first recipients of the good news of great joy concerning Jesus' birth.

God could have chosen kingly mansions in which to make a grand declaration of the divine gift. God could have gone on a gossipy Palestinian cable television program and caused quite a stir with a sensationalist host. God could have used the religious establishment and a high-toned campaign of evangelistic fervor to spread the news of the arrival of the long-awaited Messiah. God could have chosen to show up at Rome, the seat of all political power at that time, to say that the real, actual, "sure-enough," all-commanding, five-star general of all time had appeared and was ready, not merely to review the troops, but to take over their command!

Yes, we believe, God, in holy omnipotence, *could* have chosen any of those all-potent options. But the God of all surprises, who continuously blew away the expectations of all the righteous forebears – including Abraham, Isaac, Jacob, et al. – overturned everyone's expectations.

The first "you's" – "you all" if you're from the South, "you'se guys" if you're from the North – were "certain poor shepherds" on lonely hillsides, often times despairing, frequently afraid, normally wary of anything out-of-the-ordinary and consistently cautious about and focused on their charge. Certainly not privileged. Obviously poor and struggling. And unto these God gives the first announcement of the birth of the Savior of humanity.

This is a saving gift for us, I believe, for if God chose to first come unto the likes of them, then maybe – no certainly!! – God also chooses to come unto the likes of us. The logic of love which God uses in this holy equation for the reconciliation of the world to himself is this: *the only way to make it to the highest possibilities for humanity's sake, is to begin at their lowest actualities.* The only way to get to the highest is to go through the lowest.

In still other words, we can imagine God thinking, "*The big shots think they're capable of saving themselves, and defining their destiny alone. I would do better to seek out folks who've been down so long they have no place to go but up. Yeah, the shepherds will do...*" And so, not only to shepherds and to all the rest of humanity back then, but also now, to shepherds and all the rest of the current crop of humanity comes the Lord Christ. The arrival of this gift "unto you..." is an overwhelming and beautiful treasure: this one shall be called "Wonderful Counselor, Mighty God, Everlasting Father, Prince of Peace."

"Unto you..." Do you hear it?

"Unto *you*." Unto the least of these in our midst here at church, outside on the street, along the blustery roads of the whole world comes the gift of the birth of Christ.

"Unto *you*." Unto the alcoholic who appears to have lost all hope, whose feet are covered and caked with the mud of his own mediocrity, who knows that nothing can save him except that Higher Power—"Unto you is born this day in the city of David a Savior..."

"Unto *you*." Unto the a homeless person, bereft of any kind of shelter, including the most important sort, namely that of a community's embrace, unto you is born a shelter from all storms, a giver of graces upon graces, a provider of life and hope and love, so that you don't have to be without a community of welcome ever again.

"Unto *you*." Unto a career counselor, say, after another day of ceaseless streams of case after case of folks seeking out your help, after struggling with your own depression, after battling your own waywardness and indeterminate gloom—unto you is born a "Wonderful Counselor" who will soothe your worries and lighten your burdens.

"Unto *you*." Unto a person wrestling with chronic depression and constant myopia, who has read every self-help book on the top 100 list, cover to cover, who has felt that your vote doesn't really count, that your credit is always on shaky ground, that your name doesn't have hardly any pull in the community–unto you is born a "Mighty God," whose power will transform your direction and liberate you to possibilities that you've never dreamed of for yourself, for your friends, and for your family.

"Unto *you*." Unto an erring orphan who's never felt like you fit in, (so you've flitted from one relationship to another, one job to the next, embracing a life-in-the-fast-lane, hell's-bells, feet-don't-fail-me-now, head-on-dead-end-hedonism–unto you is born an "Everlasting Father," whose loving embrace is always dependable, never failing, ever-present, totally 100 percent reliable, now and forever more!

"Unto *you*." Unto all the inhabitants of Bosnia, Beijing, Beirut, and unto you, all the inhabitants of Brooklyn, Boston, Brownsville, Texas, and unto you all boys & girls, ladies & gentlemen, "friends, Romans & countrymen" of Kansas City, those who live in houses of poverty and those who live in mansions impoverished by lovelessness, those who are clad only in a T-shirt on a cold winter's night, and those who shiver in their isolation beneath the warmth of their Alaskan furs–"unto you" is born this day in the city of David, a Savior who shall be called the "Prince of Peace." Peace for your souls, peace for the rat-race of your business, peace for your family, peace for your community, peace for your schools, peace in the midst of your drudgery, peace in the midst of confusion, peace smack dab in the middle of your life, ever here, ever available, ever calming.

"Unto *you*." Two little words which make all the words which we might ever say bear something approaching eternal meaning. It is true, believe it or not. This is what the incarnation is all about.

Unto you and unto you and unto you and unto you and unto you and unto you... AMEN.

27

A Kansas City Christmas

Texts: Luke 2:1-20 and Matthew 1:1-25

There is another version of the Christmas story. It is a Kansas City version. Not all the facts in it are exactly clear, but I believe the truth of it. And the story goes like this...

There once was a couple engaged to be married. Their names were Jody and Maryanne. Maryanne came from Chanute, Kansas. And Jody came from Buffalo (Kansas). People wondered if anything good could really come from those towns. But, lo and behold, there was something good to come from those little hamlets. From Buffalo and Chanute came Jody and Maryanne. They came to Kansas City, to find a life together and to give birth.

The birth was to be a special birth. They had been visited by an angelic presence which had said to them: "Go, to Kansas City. Go, and behold the light. And take these clues with you: 'Freedom.' 'An old Mary.' And 'Three Lutherans." Look for these signs and you will find where you are to give birth to the Savior. Lo and behold, you are to be the family that ushers in the Savior."

Not wanting to argue with the angelic presence, they headed off for Kansas City. They looked for a light, and something called "freedom" and for "an old Mary" and for "three Lutherans," asking about these signs as they went along. When they reached the edge of the city, they found a light. They could see its glow hovering there over the center of the metropolis. They went to it as quickly as they could in their broken down old three-door Dodge, which sort of clunked along. Finally, they rolled into a place called the Country Club Plaza. They looked for an old Mary and three Lutherans. But no one (old or young) would claim the name Mary and no one would own up to being Lutheran. They looked for freedom, pretty much in vain. They weren't very sure about anyone having much freedom. There was only this bright gathering of lights, so they went on.

So Jody and Maryanne headed north and kept on going and found a string of lights that reached toward the heavens. They were like the Christmas lights on Christmas trees. These lights could be seen for miles and miles on a clear night. 'Was this it?' they wondered. No. It was a media transmitting tower–KCMO. This wasn't the sign they were looking for. And neither had they found any Mary or even one Lutheran. And neither did they secure anything that would point to freedom.

Jody and Maryanne journeyed on and on. And suddenly here it was. Here was the light the angelic presence had told them about. It was flickering, delicate flame on top of something called the "Liberty Memorial." And nearby was an old Mary and the Three Lutherans. There was "St. Mary's" hospital and "Trinity Lutheran" hospital. They suddenly understood that they had been instructed to look for hospitals, instead of people. This must have been it! These places would surely take this unlikely "holy" family in, so that they could give birth to the one who was to be the Savior.

Lo and behold, there was no room at the hospitals. The hospitals, like all the others in the city had experienced budget cutbacks, and there had been employee strikes in all the hospitals all across the city. To top it all off a huge blizzard had kept many of the doctors and nurses from coming in for their duties. The hospitals had to turn Jody and Maryanne away. Only a life-and-death matter would qualify them for admission. Since Maryanne wasn't in labor they couldn't take her in. So they continued to wander.

Meanwhile, three wise men from the east had heard from an angelic presence, as well. They had been given their own watchword to go to Kansas City. The names of the wise men were Tom, Peter, and Dan. They were considered wise above all others. Everybody hung on their every word. They were the shamans of the culture. They merely reported what they saw going on, but everybody thought they were predicting the future. What they reported were called "broadcasts." They communicated with those less wise via a little grey screen on a little box. The three wise men could be found on millions of little grey screens every evening. Shimmering with light, they would begin their reporting–Tom speaking his truth, Peter speaking his truth, and Dan speaking his truth.

When the three wise men were told to go to Kansas City, they were also told to keep it to themselves. They were warned not to tell the network executives nor any of the secret agents that so profusely populated Washington, DC.

Given the visitation from the angelic presence, the three wise men were just busting to tell someone. They probed around among the intelligence community: "Do you know anything about a big light or the birth of some kind of special child?" The secret agents were very interested in this rumor. They told the wise men: "When you find this special one, report back to us so we can come to see the child, too."

The wise men went, but they thought they'd better not show up empty-handed. So they toted some presents with them as they headed for Kansas City.

Meanwhile, in Grandview Missouri, just outside the Kansas City city limits, certain members of the Sanders family were visited by an angelic presence. They were told to find a light in Kansas City and to behold a special child.

The Sanders family was appropriately named, since they served as the "sanders" for the road crews when it snowed. There were three principal "sanders" among the Sanders family. Their names were Bonnie, Bounty, and Bowie. And it was to these three that the angelic presence made itself known.

Bonnie smiled all the time. To Bonnie, everything looked great and felt fine and was so sweet and nice. Her gladness at the world was a sort of unknowing happiness, though, since Bonnie didn't exactly understand the reason for her own smiling. She just knew that this was the way some folks said she ought to be. She enjoyed pleasing others, so she smiled all the time.

Bounty labored under the weight of his own name. In fact, he had lived it out. He and his wife had seven children. Under the bounteous responsibilities of his family, he was besieged with all kinds of bills.

And, Bowie? Bowie was kind of dull, never to be mistaken for a rocket scientist. He was also rather embittered, because he didn't know exactly what to do with himself. The "whys" and "wherefores" of life escaped Bowie.

During heavy snowstorms, all three of the Sanders – Bonnie, Bounty, and Bowie – came from Grandview to clean up the

Kansas City streets, so that people there could drive their cars and get to work and other important places. Out in Grandview, in the suburbs, people knew better than to try to do that. In Grandview, when a big snow came, it was a wholesale holiday for everybody. That way folks stayed safe, warm, and dry. Then they'd wait until it melted to go outside. In the suburbs, people had sense. But the folks of urban Kansas City just had to have their roads cleared.

As they were bid to do, the Sanders went into Kansas City to search for the special light that would lead them to the special child. And they did indeed find the light. They saw the flickering flame on top of the Liberty Memorial, but they didn't find the holy family. Within the shadow of the memorial, however, they thought they detected a direction to go. So they headed northeast toward a big Boulevard.

At the end of the shadow, right as it reached Southwest Boulevard, they found the special child. Jody and Maryanne had found a place that would take them in: "Manny's Mexican Food Restaurant." Since it was night, and having the usual hungry crowds gulping down the good chow, there hadn't been much that the owners could offer the family in the way of accommodations. But they did give them some tamales. And they told them that they could stay out in the garage around back, behind the restaurant.

The wise men from the east had somehow found the place, too. The garage had a kind of glow about it, like in a fantasy film or a science fiction movie. The wise men and the Sanders sensed at Manny's the same sort of wonder that they sensed when the angelic presence had spoken to them.

And so there they all were. Three "anchors" from the network news programs and three members of the road crew from Kansas City's Metropolitan Transit Authority. And what do you think happened to each of them?

The wise men proffered their gifts. Tom gave his gift: a gold Rolex. Peter offered his gift, as well: a Mercedes Benz. And Dan brought "Frank's Sauce," which, technically speaking, was actually called "Frank's Famous Barbecue Sauce," but it was commonly known as "Frank's Sauce."

The Rolex was tendered to the baby. The Mercedes Benz was pulled up right near the garage so the whole family could see it. And "Frank's Sauce" was placed right next to the lettuce crate which had been used for the baby's bed. (Dan, being a barbecue aficionado, had brought a case of it. As he put it, "As my predecessor used to say, 'That's the way it is, December 24, 1992!'–A baby ought to start off right in this world!")

How did the Sanders respond to the event? They were in awe of it all.

Bonnie was smiling. She just smiled and smiled and smiled. But now Bonnie's beaming was not an unknowing sort of smiling. She knew! She knew, now, the reason why she and other folks should smile, at the very least, once in a while. She knew, too, that she didn't need to please everybody. That wasn't the reason she was smiling now. No, she was smiling because she knew, in her head and in her heart, that she was to be pleased, that the meaning of this special child was that all people were to be pleased.

Bounty? Bounty just stood there with his mouth open. He'd never seen a baby as quiet as this special child in his whole life! He had had seven screaming little creatures all around him all of his adult life and here was this quiet child. He couldn't believe his ears!

Then there was Bowie. Bowie was weeping and weeping and weeping. Weeping, because in the child's face he saw serenity and in the mother's face he saw happiness and in the father's face he saw a purpose. In this little family, poor though they were–like hayseeds from the hinterlands of Kansas, come to Kansas City, Missouri in a beat up old Dodge–they gave him pause. They calmed him. They granted him a bit of gladness. And suddenly he knew there was a purpose, somehow, to what he was doing and what he would do in the future. He knew that throwing the sand on the street and salting the sidewalks had a reason, and that he could do his job with great joy, so that people could enjoy life. At least the folks who'd drive and walk where he had sanded and salted the good ground, at least they would be able to enjoy life a little bit more because of him. And Bonnie wept. He wept and wept and wept...

What did the holy family do? They received the gifts and enjoyed them. But they had different uses for the gifts than had been intended. Jody and Maryanne sold the gold Rolex. With the money from the sale of the Rolex they opened up a new wing at St. Mary's hospital and another one at Trinity Lutheran, for any and all families who might be found in emergency situations, so that babies could be born in peace and health.

They gave the Mercedes to the Sanders family. Thereafter, whenever the Sanders sanded the streets, they were known as the "superior Sanders." The Sanders even managed to manifest what they liked to think was a "superior driving" technique as they trekked across Kansas City and all through Grandview.

The best gift of all was the barbecue sauce. The holy family was thrilled with this gift. With it they organized a couple of beautiful banquets back in their home towns–Buffalo and Chanute. And there was great, great feasting. This was a harbinger of things to come, a foretaste of many feasts. The little child, this Savior, people would understand later, had come for just that purpose–for feasting with all people throughout all time.

By the way, Jody and Maryanne named the child "Manny," after the restaurant, of course. This was a good and right thing to do, since "Manny" was short for the Spanish word "Manuel" which the angelic presence had told the family to use for the child in the first place: "Emmanuel, or God-with-us."

Now that's the Kansas City version of the Christmas story. As I said before, not all the facts of this story are exactly clear to me, but I believe the truth of it.

Please note two qualities about "A Kansas City Christmas."

(1) This is a Christmas Eve sermon. More importantly, it is an orally oriented Christmas Eve sermon. That is to say, this sermon possesses a "spoken" quality rather than a "literary" quality. This is natural since it was intended for a specific preaching event.

(2) Since a speaking event always includes two parties – speaker(s) and listener(s) – remember that a sermon always has a congregation. People who congregate at churches always respond to what is being said, either demonstrably or imperceptibly. But they respond nevertheless. I regret that sermon readers do not have the experience of "being there" like preaching hearers do. But maybe there is a kind of response that even readers can make. May you, kind reader, respond to all your Christmas experiences with unmitigated joy and graceful abandon.

Prayers

28

Benediction, Urban League of GKC

47th Annual Difference Maker Luncheon

Loving and Giving God–
You are the giver of
justice and generosity,
reconciliation and righteousness,
transformation and truth.
And You are One who ultimately and finally keeps all holy appointments. How glad we are for this appointment with You this day. And how fortunate we have been that You have kept Your appointments with us
for equality's sake,
for compassion's sake,
for dignity's sake.
Hear our gratitude for this meal and our fellowship today.
But keep us keenly attuned now and in the near and far future to the appointments You have set for us,
appointments with the keepers of the gates of opportunity,
appointments with the children and youth in our communities,

appointments with civic and religious and cultural leaders who want to do good for all people.

And wake us up, and stir us on until we keep all of our appointments with Your divine intentions for all of the human family.

Dazed and dazzled by all of Your grace,
amazed by Your provision,
inspired by Your holy presence, and
Earnest to keep our appointments with You as You have kept Your appointments with us,
we pray this in Your Holy Name. AMEN.

29

9-11 Memorial Invocation

Bless this day, O God of the plains,
God of the mountains,
God of the flint hills and muddy rivers,
Cosmic Creator and Righteous Ruler of the seas,
Giver of all graces and truth and hope and dreams,
O precious Holy One, bless this day
    and bless the days we remember,
        with tearful attention
            and silent honoring and fervent hope.
Make your way plain this morning, O God,
    that children are precious,
    that families are treasures,
        that friends and neighbors and fellow citizens
        are like kindred and should be honored as such
        in any community worthy of the name called "home."
Heal our hearts, gracious God; heal them with a fierce love,
cauterize our woundedness,

assuage our pain,
soothe our anger,
calm any and all fears,
as we remember the sacred ones, gone now,
those whose lives honor our lives
with their legacy of caring love
and their deathless devotion to freedom.
Abide with us, too, we pray this morning,
in the beauty of open, free skies.
Grant us renewed minds and refreshed souls
and a far-reaching vision,
so that the work to which we set our hands
and the dreams to which we commit our souls
shall be noble blessings
for those yet to be born in this land and
those born upon any soil
in any place where courageous people yearn for justice,
live by mercy,
and endure in peace
through love and loyalty.
And as we behold flags unfurled
and listen to bells tolled with tender respect,
as we cling to each other in undying love
—hand in hand, arm in arm, heart to heart—
hear us as we say our prayers,
immigrants and homesteaders,
rich and poor,
outcasts and privileged,
liberal and conservative and moderate,
leaders and followers,
multilingual and monolingual,
red and yellow,

black and white,
and tan and brown,
Chippewa and Cherokee,
Ute and Sioux,
Kiowa and Iriquoi,
Christians and Jews and Muslims,
Buddhists and Hindus and Sikhs and B'hais,
and all the rest of the array of Your one human family.
Hear us as we utter our prayers,
however we call Your name,
which,
among all our words,
is the holiest of all. AMEN.

30

Closing Prayer

Yad Vashem Holocaust Memorial –

Jerusalem Gathering 2006

"Valley of the Communities" Prayer Service

Gracious Creator, Lord of Life, God of our fathers and mothers –
What language shall we borrow
to come before Your throne of grace and
to say what we feel on this sacred ground?
What words are adequate and eligible
to sum up our awe and astonishment and horror
as we remember?
You alone have the power
to intercede for us,
to lift our faltering speech,
to give wings to our prayers,
to quicken our hearts and minds and souls
to take up the tasks set to our hands.
You, above all, have the power
(with sighs too deep for words)

to help us to pray.
Here us as we confess:
The good we would have done,
we did not do.
The evil we would never have done
is the very thing we did
or we allowed to happen
or we forgot
or we did not care
or we did not care enough.
Hear us as we engage that most sacred of human callings—memory—
remembering the lives and the loss of the millions,
remembering the cost to the world,
remembering the eyes and the dreams,
remembering the hands and the promise,
remembering the families and the years.
Give us grace and hearts strong enough
to say with conviction and without equivocation:
We know Your calling to us now, this day, in this place—
treading the land where Abraham bound Isaac,
walking where Jesus walked,
recalling those who were taken from the world
but whose legacy can not, should not ever
be forgotten—
We are here, here,
now,
and we are not leaving. AMEN.

TIMES AND PLACES

The moment and the actual circumstances for preaching any sermon or offering any prayer are crucially important. Another way of emphasizing this truth is to say that there really are no effective sermons and prayers which are "timeless" or "for all humanity." Sermons and prayers do their most lasting, powerful work when they are locatable in time and in connection with a particular congregation or a specific occasion. Sermons and prayers may – and indeed should – touch upon eternal verities and deathless dreams, but they always exist "for a moment." Thus it is thought that an indication of the times and places for the efforts in this volume might be valuable to the reader.

Most of the sermons in this collection were first offered at Community Christian Church, at the corner of 46th and Main, in Kansas City, Missouri. Some have found "legs" and have gone traveling, being preached in multiple venues. Those sermons are *"What Then Shall We Say,"* *"A Way Out of No Way,"* *"One Little Word,"* *"Shhh...,"* *When Second Best Is Better,""Things I Know Now That I Wish Knew Then,."* and *"A Kansas City Christmas."* The times and places indicated for these particular sermons are either the earliest or the most recent dates and locations.

1– Living Beyond Fear: An Open Letter to the Candidates
September 26, 2004, Community Christian Church, Kansas City, Missouri

2– The Gospel and the Da Vinci Code
February 29, 2004, Community Christian Church, Kansas City, Missouri

3– The Resurrection and The Life: Easter
April 16, 2006, Community Christian Church, Kansas City, Missouri

4– Columbine: Crisis & Christ in Colorado
May 2, 1999, Community Christian Church, Kansas City, Missouri

5– Overcoming the Church's Biggest Crisis
June 1, 2003, Community Christian Church, Kansas City, Missouri

6– Peace and The Prophet's Heart
December 31, 2005, Rime Buddhist Center, Kansas City, Missouri

7– What Then Shall We Say (The 5 Things A Minister Has to Say)
June 25, 2006, Community Christian Church, Kansas City, Missouri

8– A Way Out of No Way
November 12, 2006, Covenant Christian Church, Cary, North Carolina

9– One Little Word
March 4, 2003, DeKalb Christian Church, DeKalb, Missouri

10–The Gospel & 'The Passion of The Christ'
March 28, 2004, Community Christian Church, Kansas City, Missouri

11–Shhh... (A Baccalaureate Sermon)
May 14, 2006, Stone Chapel, Drury University, Springfield, Missouri

12–Of Callings, Canyons, & Christian Enduring
June 6, 2004, Community Christian Church, Kansas City, Missouri

13–When Second Best Is Better
August 11, 2002, Community Christian Church, Kansas City, Missouri

14–Training Up the Wise Child
February 4, 2007, Community Christian Church, Kansas City, Missouri

15–How to Negate Negativity
May 14, 1995, Community Christian Church, Kansas City, Missouri

16–Architecture of the Spirit
May 7, 1995, Community Christian Church, Kansas City, Missouri

17–Things I Know Now That I Wish Knew Then
August 24, 2004, Shawnee Mission Medical Center, Shawnee Mission, Kansas

18–The Touch
February 28, 2001, Community Christian Church, Kansas City, Missouri

19–The Answer in the Ashes
February 13, 2002, Community Christian Church, Kansas City, Missouri

20–Grace for the Left-Overs
March 5, 2003, Community Christian Church, Kansas City, Missouri

21–When Grace Gets Real
February 25, 2004, Community Christian Church, Kansas City, Missouri

22–Worth the Waiting
February 9, 2005, Community Christian Church, Kansas City, Missouri

23–Who Is He, Really?
March 1, 2006, Community Christian Church, Kansas City, Missouri

24–Candles of Grace
December 24, 2004, Community Christian Church, Kansas City, Missouri

25–The Holly of Hope on Christmas Day
December 25, 2005, Community Christian Church, Kansas City, Missouri

26–Unto You
December 23, 1993, Community Christian Church, Kansas City, Missouri

27–A Kansas City Christmas
December 19, 2001, Community Christian Church, Kansas City, Missouri

28–Benediction, Urban League of GKC
Dec. 9, 2004, Hyatt Regency Hotel, Crown Center, Kansas City, Missouri

29–9-11 Memorial Invocation
September 11, 2003, Johnson County Courtyard, Olathe, Kansas

30–Closing Prayer, Yad Vashem Holocaust Memorial
Friday, January 13, 2006, 5766, Valley of the Communities, Yad Vashem, Jerusalem, Israel

About the Author

Born in Honolulu, Hawaii, raised in Texas, seasoned in Los Angles, California, and Nashville, Tennessee, Dr. Robert Lee Hill has served, since 1987, as senior minister of the Community Christian Church in Kansas City, Missouri.

Prior to his undergraduate and graduate studies, he was a conscientious objector during the war in Viet Nam and served for two years as a youth and family worker at All Peoples Christian Center in south-central Los Angeles. Before arriving in Kansas City, Dr. Hill served with a nonprofit agency working with ex-prisoners and their families.

Dr. Hill holds a B.A. degree from Texas Christian University, an M.Div. degree from Vanderbilt University Divinity School, and a D.D. from Christian Theological Seminary. He has spoken as a keynoter and guest preacher at seminaries, assemblies, clergy meetings, retreats, conferences, and congregations across the United States in a wide array of Christian, Jewish and interfaith venues.

Since 1993, Dr. Hill has been a co-host of the renowned Sunday morning radio call-in show, *"Religion on the Line,"* on KCMO-Talk Radio 710AM.

Dr. Hill's articles, essays, and poems have appeared in national magazines and periodicals. For four years (1997-2001) he was a monthly columnist for *The Disciple* magazine. Among the works he has written or edited are ***Made Whole Again...***; ***By Broken Bread: A Devotional Guide Through the Gospel of Luke***; ***Empowering Congregations: Successful Strategies for 21st Century Leadership*** (with Denton L. Roberts); and ***Hard To Tell: A Congregations of Poems, 1990-2003***. This is his eighth book.

Dr. Hill is married to Priscilla Reckling, and they live in the Brookside neighborhood in Kansas City, Missouri.

Additional copies of this book may be obtained from your bookstore or by contacting **Hope Publishing House,** P.O. Box 60008, Pasadena, CA 91116 - U.S.A.
(626) 792-6123 / (800) 326-2671; Fax (626) 792-2121
www.hope-pub.com; E-mail: hopepub@sbcglobal.net